FIDELER SOCIAL STUDIES

Families
Family life: sharing, caring, and working together
A Chartbook of discussion pictures

Families Around the World
How families live in communities around the world.

Our Needs
The needs of people in families and in communities

Our Earth
Our Earth, its geography, its people and communities.

Great Americans and Great Ideas
Biographies of thirteen great Americans.
The great ideas that built our nation.

The United States
The people, geography, and history of the United States. The Northeast, The South, Midwest and Great Plains, The West, Pictorial Story of Our Country. Depth Studies.

American Neighbors
The people, geography, and history of Canada, Mexico, Caribbean Lands, and South America. Depth Studies.

World Cultures
The people, geography, and history of ten world regions. British Isles, Germany, France, Soviet Union, China, Japan, India, Southeast Asia, Africa, South America. Depth Studies.

Inquiring About Freedom
United States history. Depth Studies of the ''freedom'' concepts that built our nation.

Jerry E. Jennings

Jerry E. Jennings is an author and editor of textbooks for young people. He received his education at Michigan State University and Columbia University. Mr. Jennings has traveled widely throughout the United States and has done extensive research in the field of American history.

Tom Lee

Tom Lee is an author and editor of numerous books and articles on history, art, and science. He has traveled widely throughout the United States, Africa, and Europe. Mr. Lee's experiences as a teacher and visiting lecturer in the social sciences have helped him to communicate with young people in a meaningful way.

Margaret Fisher Hertel

Margaret Fisher Hertel is an author and editor of books for children. After graduating from Maryville College in Tennessee, she continued her education at Mexico City College. As a teacher and a parent, Mrs. Hertel is keenly aware of the needs and interests of our country's students.

Contributors to Great Americans and Great Ideas

R. DALE BELLINO
Principal
Greater Plains Elementary School
Oneonta, New York

GEORGE F. CARTER
Distinguished Professor of Geography
Texas A & M University
College Station, Texas

ROBERT E. CONNORS
Chairman, Department
of Elementary Education
Edinboro State College
Edinboro, Pennsylvania

ALEXANDER DeCONDE
Professor of History
University of California
Santa Barbara, California

DOROTHY McCLURE FRASER
Social Science Coordinator
Teacher Education Program
Hunter College
New York, New York

PAUL WALLACE GATES
Professor Emeritus, Department
of History
Cornell University
Ithaca, New York

CATHERINE E. GOODRICH
Instructional Supervisor
Oakwood School
Ramapo District No. 2
Spring Valley, New York

DON E. HAMACHEK
Professor of Educational Psychology
Michigan State University
East Lansing, Michigan

FLORENCE JACKSON
Director, Center for the Humanities
and the Arts
New York City Public Schools
New York, New York

HELEN McGINNIS
Consultant in Education
Sacramento County Schools
Sacramento, California

G. ETZEL PEARCY
Chairman, Department of Geography
California State College at Los Angeles
Los Angeles, California

ROBERT B. RUDDELL
Acting Dean, School of Education
University of California
Berkeley, California

GEORGE D. SPINDLER
Professor of Anthropology
Stanford University
Stanford, California

ELAINE STOWE
Program Specialist, Language Arts
Sacramento City Unified School District
Curriculum Development Center
Sacramento, California

BETTY-JO BUELL

MARGARET S. DeWITT

MARY A. DOWNEY

EVELYN M. DOWNING

RAYMOND E. FIDELER

MARY JANE FOWLER

SUSAN R. GROOVER

BARBARA LaBELLE

MARY MITUS

BETTY MORIARTY

VIRGINIA A. SKALSKY

BARBARA M. SMITH

MARION H. SMITH

WILL STRAND

JUDY A. TAYLOR

AUDREY WITHAM

JOANNA VAN ZOEST

GREAT AMERICANS
AND
GREAT IDEAS

Jennings, Lee , Hertel

LIBRARY OF CONGRESS CATALOG CARD NUMBER: 78-54257
ISBN: 0-88296-483-6

THE FIDELER COMPANY   GRAND RAPIDS, MICHIGAN • TORONTO, CANADA

Contents

Great Americans

Great Ideas

Thinking Aids

A great statesman. Benjamin Franklin was our country's first minister* to France. He was also an author, inventor, and scientist.* Benjamin Franklin did much to help our country grow. He started a school and a library. He was also in charge of the post offices for all the colonies.*

1 Benjamin Franklin

One summer afternoon about 260 years ago, Ben Franklin ran down the stairs of his home in Boston, Massachusetts. Under his arm were two small wooden paddles which he had just finished making.

"Where are you going?" called his mother.

*See Glossary

b. 1706   d. 1790

1700   1800   1900   2000

"Down to the pond to try out an idea," Ben answered.

When he reached the pond, Ben quickly undressed. He picked up a paddle in each hand. Then he waded into the water. Ben leaned forward and began to swim. The paddles pushed strongly against the water. They made his arms tired, but he didn't care. The paddles helped him to swim much faster. His idea was working!

Ben liked to think and try out his ideas. He liked to find answers to questions that always filled his mind. Surely there wasn't another boy in Boston so full of questions.

Ben wanted more time for reading and learning. Instead, he had to spend most of his days earning a living. Ben was the fifteenth child in a family of seventeen. Mr. Franklin knew that young Ben had a keen, questioning mind. But he could only pay for about two years of school for Ben. After that, the boy had to go to work in the family candle shop. Making candles was dull work for a bright boy like Ben. He became so restless that Mr. Franklin was afraid he would run away to sea.

When Ben was twelve, he became an apprentice* in his brother James' printing shop. There was more

Philadelphia printer. As a boy, Ben Franklin worked in his brother's printing shop.

chance to learn in the print shop than in the candle shop. Ben was much happier. He read and thought about the stories which he helped to print in his brother's newspaper. Then he wrote some stories of his own. Ben knew that James would not print these if he discovered that his younger brother was the author. So he signed them "Mrs. Silence Dogood." Then he slipped them under the door of the print shop at night. James thought these stories were very good and printed them.

At seventeen, he ran away to Philadelphia. Later, Ben opened his own printing shop.

He was angry, however, when he found out who the real author was.

When Ben was seventeen, he ran away from Boston and went to Philadelphia. He had hardly a penny to his name. However, he had a good mind, and he dared to try out his ideas. By the time he was twenty-four, he had a print shop of his own.

Franklin had the busiest print shop in Philadelphia. However, he was interested in much more than business. For one thing, he liked to write. Each year, for twenty-five years, he wrote and printed a book called *Poor Richard's Almanac*. These books told about the weather and tides. They also had cooking ideas, poems, and calendars. Many wise and funny sayings which Franklin made up himself were printed in the books.

Ben Franklin was also interested in people. In Philadelphia, he formed a club where he and his friends could gather to talk about important matters. This later became the American Philosophical Society.*

As a man, Franklin still liked to read and try out ideas. He taught himself to read books written in many languages. He also carried out several important experiments.* In one of these, he proved that lightning is electricity. This made him known all over Europe as well as in America.

Franklin used his many ideas to help other people. Through his club, he helped to improve the Philadelphia police department. He also helped to start the first fire department in the city. Franklin helped to start the first hospital in Pennsylvania. Because he felt that learning was so important, he started the first lending library in the colonies.* He also founded a school that later became the University of Pennsylvania. To make life safer and easier for other people, Franklin invented* several useful things. Among these were the lightning* rod, the Franklin* stove, and bifocal* glasses. It is not surprising that Franklin became one of the best-loved citizens of Philadelphia.

Franklin's interests then spread to America as a whole. When he was forty-two, he retired from business. Then he spent most of his time in public service. He served the post

A famous experiment.* In 1752 Ben Franklin proved that lightning is electricity. Throughout his life he tried many different experiments. He also invented many useful things. Can you name any of them? Are any of his inventions still used today?

office at Philadelphia. Later he was in charge of the post offices for all of the colonies.

About this time, England and France were at war. The French were asking the Indians to attack the English colonists on the frontier.*

Franklin tried to get the different colonies to work together to protect themselves against these attacks. But they would not listen to him. He then helped to raise armies to defend the colonists. He also was in charge of building a fort.

Franklin was also worried about the way the British government was treating the American colonies. Before the Revolutionary War,* he was sent to England twice to help straighten out the troubles between the colonies and the English government. At first, he did not feel that it was important for the colonies to become independent.* He did feel that they should be treated fairly by the English government. Franklin did get the English to remove a heavy tax that was brought about by the Stamp Act.* However, he finally decided that England would never treat the colonies as her equals. When he returned to America in 1775, he entered into his country's fight for freedom. He was one of the five men who prepared the Declaration of Independence.*

During and after the Revolutionary War, Benjamin Franklin served his country as minister* to France. He won the love of many people in that country. He asked the French leaders to give the colonists guns and food. They agreed.

Franklin was a very old man when he returned to America. But his days of service were not over. He worked with the men who wrote our country's Constitution.* Later he became the president* of the first anti-slavery* society in America.

To the end of his life, this great American served his country. He helped to make life better for other people.

- Name several things Benjamin Franklin invented.
- What did Benjamin Franklin help to write?

Language

See Great Ideas

Benjamin Franklin wrote many books. Language was very important to him. Later, Franklin helped write our country's Declaration of Independence.* To do this, he needed to know the meanings of words and how to use them. Language is also important to you. How could you communicate* with your family or friends if you could not speak or write clearly?

A young general. George Washington served as commander of our country's first army. Later, he became our first president.* George Washington helped to create our government.

2 George Washington

The hot June sun beat down on a disorderly column of running soldiers. Shouts filled the dusty, summer air. The officers in charge were not trying to gather together the fleeing army. Each man was looking out for himself. Suddenly, a white horse carrying a tall rider galloped to the top of the hill toward which the men were running.

*See Glossary

b. 1732　　　　d. 1799

1700　　　　1800　　　　1900　　　　2000

"Look! It's General Washington!" shouted one soldier. The news flashed back from man to man. As if by magic, the soldiers halted. The noise died down. Quietly, the soldiers turned back to face the enemy. Once again, George Washington had kept the American army together. As in the past, his leadership had brought his country one step closer to winning the Revolutionary War.*

People who knew young George Washington never dreamed he would grow up to be a great leader. He was a shy boy who loved sports and games. Much of his time was spent riding horseback. He liked to hunt and swim near his father's Virginia home. However, this quiet boy was sensible and dependable. He also worked hard. Perhaps this was why people liked him. They felt they could trust him.

One person who was very fond of George was his oldest half brother, Lawrence. Their father died when George was eleven. Lawrence tried to be like a father to his younger brother. He invited George to live with him at his home, "Mount Vernon." Here, George met many interesting, educated people. From them he learned many things that would help him in life. Later, Lawrence hired two people to teach George military skills, such as leading men in battle. He also learned quiet, good manners. He stood straight and tall as soldiers do. He became the kind of young man that people looked up to.

Surveying* land on the frontier.* George Washington surveyed land in the wilderness. He learned how to live in harsh conditions.

The French and Indian War.* Young George Washington helped save many soldiers during a terrible battle. General Braddock* was wounded. The soldiers were without a leader. George Washington took command. He led the soldiers to safety. People admired George Washington's courage.*

Another man who liked and helped young Washington was a wealthy neighbor. This was Lord Thomas Fairfax. When George was sixteen, Lord Fairfax thought he was dependable enough to help survey* some lands on the frontier.* George did his work so well that he was given the job of public surveyor. As he did this work, he learned much about life in the frontier forests. George also showed that he could put up with the hardships of the frontier.

Soon young Washington received a great honor. He was asked to serve as an aide to General Braddock,* the British commander in the French and Indian War.* During a terrible battle, General Braddock was wounded. His soldiers were frightened. Courageously,* young Washington helped to gather the soldiers together. He led them to safety. After this battle, people in the colonies* could see that George Washington was a leader. They could depend on him.

Washington served as commander of the Virginia soldiers for about three years. In 1759 he returned to Mount Vernon, which he had inherited* from his half brother Lawrence. Here, he spent the days watching over the work on his large farms. With his wife, Martha, he enjoyed the company of many guests. Washington would have been happy to spend the rest of his life at Mount Vernon. However, it soon became clear that the Revolutionary War could not be avoided. He felt that he must leave his home to help his country in its fight for freedom.

Washington joined the other colonial leaders at the Second Continental Congress* in Philadelphia. The men around him remembered his courage and leadership in the French and Indian War. On June 15, 1775, they elected* him commander in chief of the Continental Army.

Washington's job was very hard. His soldiers had almost no training. Some of Washington's generals did not think that he should be in charge. Worst of all, the governments of the thirteen colonies did not work together to give him the food, clothing, and weapons he needed for his army.

The hardest months of the war came during the winter of 1777-1778. Washington was camped with his soldiers at Valley Forge, in Pennsylvania. Cold winter winds howled around the tiny log huts in which the soldiers lived. The soldiers' clothes were too worn and torn to keep them warm. Many of them did not have shoes. There was not enough food to eat. It is not surprising that some of the starving, freezing men decided to go home. If it had not been for Washington,

all of them might have left. Day after day, he rode through the camp, encouraging the soldiers. His courage kept the tired little army together. In 1781, Washington led his army to final victory over the British.

Washington's leadership was still needed after the war. The thirteen states were not yet united into one strong nation. Some Americans thought this could best be done if George Washington would become dictator* or king. Most men would have been glad to gain that much power. Washington, however, did not agree with that idea. He had

At Valley Forge. George Washington held his ragged, hungry army together during the cold winter of 1777-1778. George Washington was admired and loved by his soldiers.

fought hard for freedom. Now he worked hard to help Americans use their freedom wisely. He served as president* of the group which wrote our Constitution.* Then he was elected to be the first president of the United States. It is not surprising that we call him "The Father of His Country."

- Give some reasons why George Washington was made commander of the Continental Army.

- What kind of hardships did Washington's army experience at Valley Forge?

- Why do you think Washington did not want to become a dictator or a king?

Rules
and
Government

See Great Ideas

Our country's Constitution.* Some people wanted George Washington to become a dictator or a king. He refused. George Washington had fought hard for freedom. Now, he wanted to help people use their freedom wisely. George Washington helped to write our country's Constitution. In so doing, he helped to create our government. Later, George Washington became the first president of the United States.

The Lincoln Memorial. This memorial was built to honor Abraham Lincoln. It is located in Washington, D.C. Abraham Lincoln was our country's sixteenth president.*

3 Abraham Lincoln

Abraham Lincoln was one of our greatest Americans. He was wise enough to see what needed to be done in time of trouble. He also had the courage* to do what he saw was needed. Without this wise leader at the time of the Civil War,* the United States might have been divided into two separate countries.

Lincoln's boyhood was different from that of most of our country's leaders. He was born in a one-room

*See Glossary

b. 1809   d. 1865

1700   1800   1900   2000

log cabin in Kentucky. His father was a farmer. He moved the family to the Indiana frontier* when Abe was seven. Mr. Lincoln did not think education was important. So Abe went to school for less than a year. Instead, he spent the days helping to clear the forestland. He also helped with other farm work. When Abe was nine his mother died. Home was no longer a happy place. Young Abe and his sister Sarah gave a warm welcome to their father's new wife. She was a warm, kind person. She helped Abe to read and study at home.

Young Abe's neighbors liked him. He was much taller and stronger than most of his friends. No one in the county could beat him in a wrestling match. No one could run faster. He knew more jokes and funny stories than most people. When people gathered, he was often the center of a crowd of laughing men and boys. Much of Abe's time was spent reading books he borrowed from his neighbors. He was eager to learn.

Lincoln liked people. He learned to understand them better through the many kinds of work he did. In

Young Abraham Lincoln spent much of his time reading books which he borrowed from neighbors. Abe was eager to learn. He often read by firelight.

As a lawyer Lincoln traveled across Illinois on horseback. He practiced law in the county courts. In this way he became well known in many parts of Illinois.

Illinois, where he lived after he grew up, Lincoln worked in a store. He also was in charge of a post office. At one time, he was a member of the state legislature.* Then he taught himself law and became a good lawyer. During that time, Lincoln also served one term in the United States House of Representatives.*

Abe Lincoln was a very good lawyer, but he was mostly interested in government. He felt he could do more to help his country if he were serving in the government.

One of the very big problems in the United States at that time was slavery.* In the early years of our country, many black workers had been brought to the United States. Here they were sold to plantation* owners. They were made to work for their white masters. Slaves were owned mostly in the southern states. In the South, many workers were needed on the huge cotton plantations.

During the Civil War* Abraham Lincoln issued the Emancipation Proclamation.* How did this help the people who were slaves gain freedom?

In the North, many farms were small and there were many factories. Slaves were not needed. The northern states soon passed laws against slavery.

In Lincoln's time, many new states joined the Union.* People in the

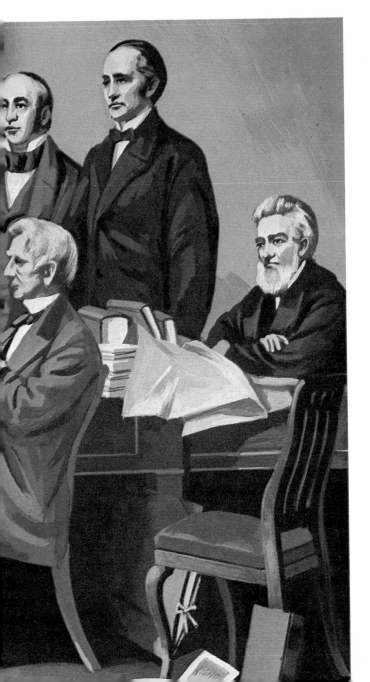

North thought slavery should not be allowed in these new states. People in the South thought it should be allowed. People in these two parts of our country could not agree.

Lincoln felt that slavery was wrong. It should not be allowed in the new states. He wanted to do something about this. In 1854 and again in 1858, he decided to run for the United States Senate.* When he ran for this office, he made many speeches. He explained his thoughts about slavery. He gave some of his best-known speeches in a series of debates* with Stephen A. Douglas. This man was running for office against Lincoln. Though Lincoln did not win either election,* his speeches made him well known all over the country. In 1860, he was chosen president* of the United States.

The people of the southern states were unhappy about Lincoln becoming president. They thought he would try to keep slavery out of the new states. They also feared that the government would pass a law against slavery in the South. To keep this from happening, many of the southern states separated from the Union.

Lincoln understood how the southern people felt. He promised not to ask for a law against slavery

Freedom

See Great Ideas

A great leader. Abraham Lincoln led our country through the Civil War. He believed that the states should be united. He worked to prevent our country from becoming many weak countries. He knew America would remain strong only when all the states were united. Abraham Lincoln told the people of the South, "We are not enemies but friends."

in the southern states. He asked that Northerners and Southerners work to keep the country together. "We are not enemies but friends," he said. "We must not be enemies."

Still, the southern states that had left the Union refused to return. They formed a separate country. It was called the Confederate States of America. A weak leader might have let them stay out. Lincoln, however, did not allow this. He knew that if these states left the Union, other states might do the same. This would break our strong country into several small, weak countries.

Lincoln did not want to fight a war to save the Union. However, once the Civil War began, he led the northern states to victory. During this terrible war, he gave an order called the Emancipation Proclamation.* This led to freedom for the slaves. Never again would the question of slavery divide the country. At last, the words "all men are created equal" were becoming more true.

In 1865, the war was over. Then Lincoln started the great task of rebuilding his country. He did not have time to finish his work, however. On the evening of April 14, he attended a play with his wife and some friends. Suddenly, a shot rang through the theater. An actor named John Wilkes Booth leaped from the President's box. He ran from the building. For a moment, no one understood what had happened. Then the terrible news swept through the room. Lincoln had been shot.

Today Americans everywhere admire Lincoln as a leader of his country.

- What offices did Abraham Lincoln hold?

- Why were the people of the South unhappy with Abraham Lincoln?

- Why did Abraham Lincoln feel the Civil War could not be avoided?

- What was the Emancipation Proclamation?

4 Chief Joseph

The Nez Percé Indians loved the Wallowa Valley. It was quiet and peaceful. It was also one of the most beautiful places in Oregon. The Nez Percés lived in small villages along several rivers in the valley. There they were free to live as they had always lived. They fished and hunted. They raised horses. They roamed the forests and plains. The Nez Percés were a gentle people. And the Wallowa Valley was a gentle place.

The Nez Percés loved Joseph, their chief, as much as they loved their home. Joseph was a strong but kindly man. He stood six feet tall. He was handsome and very able. He was also a skilled warrior. But Chief Joseph was a man of peace. He did not like war.

Joseph's people admired his courage* and strength. They also admired his love of peace.

In 1877 trouble came to Chief Joseph. For many years white settlers had moved closer and closer to the valley. They, too, thought it was a beautiful place. And they wanted it for themselves. Soldiers were sent to move the Nez Percés to a reservation* many miles away. The reservation was not as beautiful as the Wallowa Valley. It was not their home. The Nez Percés would have less freedom on the reservation.

The Nez Percés did not want to leave their home. Many braves wanted to fight the soldiers. They were willing to die for their freedom. Joseph did not want to move, either. He loved his freedom very much. Yet, he knew that many of his people would die if war started. The white soldiers were many. The Nez Percés were few. To avoid war, Joseph sadly agreed to take his people to the new reservation. Before he could do so, however, a handful of braves killed several white settlers. They did this against Joseph's wishes. Their actions caused Joseph much sadness. He did not want to kill. He did not want war.

"I would have given my own life if I could have undone the killing of white men by my people," Joseph said.

But it was too late. General Oliver Howard saw the killing as an act of war. He quickly sent soldiers to attack the Nez Percés in the Wallowa Valley. Now Joseph had no choice

*See Glossary

b. 1840   d. 1904

20 1700   1800   1900   2000

Joseph, Chief of the Nez Percés. In 1877 he led his people on a 1,600-mile journey. They traveled through rough mountain country in search of freedom. Chief Joseph cared deeply for his people. He showed all Americans the real meanings of the words loyalty* and courage.*

but to fight. He had to protect his people. He was a peaceful man. He was also a great leader, however. The soldiers had better guns than the Nez Percés. But Joseph knew the Wallowa Valley. After all, his people had lived there for many years. Under Joseph's leadership, sixty Nez Percé warriors defeated General Howard's army.

Some soldiers were wounded and captured. They were not harmed after the battle.

"We do not believe in scalping,"* Joseph said, "nor in killing wounded men."

Joseph knew that more soldiers would soon come to the valley. He also knew that his people wanted to remain free, as he did. They would not go to the reservation. Instead, Joseph led them east into Montana. He planned to lead them to Canada, where the Nez Percés could live in freedom.

Carrying what little they had, the Nez Percés began their long journey.

Some rode horses. Others walked. In Montana Joseph led his band of seven hundred into the mountains. He hoped to escape from the white soldiers. Traveling in the mountains was very hard. In fact, it was almost impossible. There were many hardships. More than half of Joseph's followers were women and children. Soon, the hardships became even worse. There was little food. The weather was colder. There were no blankets to protect the Indians from the cold and biting wind. Some children froze to death. Still, the Nez Percés followed Joseph through the mountains. They believed in him.

A long journey for freedom. The Nez Percés were seeking freedom. They fought thirteen battles with the soldiers. Time after time they escaped General Howard's well-armed troops.

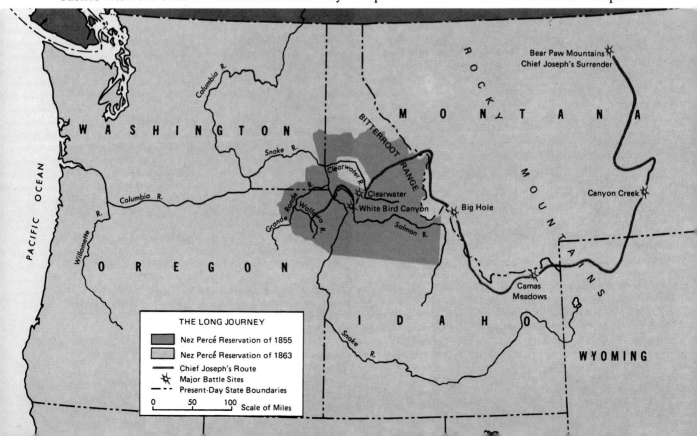

Through the mountains. In 1877 Chief Joseph led seven hundred Nez Percés on a journey to freedom. They had little food. They had no blankets. The Nez Percés were attacked by soldiers many times. Freedom was important to Chief Joseph and his people. The Nez Percés risked their lives to gain freedom. Would you do what Chief Joseph did? How important is freedom to you?

They took comfort in his strength. They knew Chief Joseph would lead them to freedom.

In eleven weeks Joseph and his people covered more than 1,600 miles of rough country. There were soldiers to fight at every turn. Joseph's braves were by now tired and hungry. Yet, they followed him into battle thirteen times against the soldiers. They won nearly every battle.

Joseph's skill and cleverness surprised the soldiers. Time after time he escaped their rifle bullets. Soon, the Nez Percés would be near freedom. Soon they would be in Canada.

However, the hard journey had weakened the Indians. They were starving and dying. The terrible cold weather only got worse. Chief Joseph wanted to go on to Canada. He wanted his people to be free. He faced a hard decision, and his heart was weary. Would he go on with the journey?

Joseph wanted no more of his people to die of hunger or cold, or from a soldier's rifle. Many of his braves were already dead.

In September, 1877, Joseph made the hardest decision of his life. His

Joseph surrenders.* He gave up his freedom so his people might live. Later, Joseph went to our nation's capital to talk about freedom.

great concern was for his people. He chose to surrender* to General Howard. He did this so his people might live. It was a sad moment. Joseph had chosen life for his people over freedom. He had stopped less than forty miles from Canada. Chief Joseph was only thirty-seven when he gave up his freedom to General Howard's soldiers.

The soldiers took everything from the Nez Percés. They had nothing left now . . . no land . . . no horses. Worse yet, they had no freedom.

Joseph later went to Washington, D.C., to talk with people in the government about his people. He spoke to them from his heart.

"Let me be a free man . . . free to travel, free to stop, free to work . . . free to think and talk and act for myself . . . and I will obey every law or submit to the penalty."

Today, Chief Joseph's great courage and leadership are an example to all people who love freedom. Joseph, of the Nez Percés, taught America the true meaning of loyalty* and courage.

- Why was freedom important to Chief Joseph?
- Did the government treat Joseph and his people fairly? Explain.

Women should have the right to vote. Susan B. Anthony worked for many years to help women gain the right to vote. She spoke to thousands of people. In 1920 Congress passed a law giving women the right to vote. Some people called this law the Susan B. Anthony Amendment.

5 Susan B. Anthony

It was a beautiful summer day in 1826. It was a wonderful day for a drive in the country. Susan Anthony was excited. She was going on a trip with her father. He was going to visit Judge McLean, a wealthy business-man. Judge McLean lived in Batten-ville, New York. Battenville was more than forty miles away from Susan's home near Adams, Massa-chusetts. She had never gone on such a long carriage ride before.

b. 1820

d. 1906

1700   1800   1900   2000

At Judge McLean's home Susan saw something that upset her. She saw people who had no freedom. They were slaves, working to earn their freedom. They were black. Susan had never seen black people before. Her father told her about slavery.* He explained how black people in the South were bought and sold. He also told her how they were forced to work. Sometimes, black children were taken away from their mothers and sold. Susan was sad. She couldn't see how anyone could treat people that way. She couldn't imagine being taken away from her family or living without her freedom. She decided that one day she would help people who did not have the freedom she had.

In 1835, when Susan was fifteen, she became a teacher. Later, she went back to school. She wanted to learn more so that she could become a better teacher. In 1838, however, she had to leave school. Her father's cotton mill had failed. There was no money to pay for the cost of going to school. To help her father, Susan began to teach again in New Rochelle, New York. She sent much of her earnings home for her family.

In New Rochelle, Susan saw racial* hatred for the first time. Several people walked out of church because a black man had come to the services. This angered Susan.

"What a lack of Christianity is this!" Susan wrote to a friend.

Perhaps it was because of this that Susan began to work against slavery. She also began to work very hard for women's* rights. At that time women did not have many freedoms. They were not allowed to vote. Married women could not own homes. If they did work, their husbands could take their earnings from them.

*See Glossary

A leader in the fight for freedom. Susan B. Anthony led the fight for women's* rights in America. In 1872 she led the first group of women to vote in a national election.*

Susan spoke to many groups about this. She was a strong and powerful speaker. She wanted to make people understand how unfair the law was to women and to others, such as blacks and Indians. It was wrong to deny anyone their freedom.

Susan was often laughed at for her beliefs. Some people insulted her. But a few listened. Even though her beliefs were not popular, she refused to stop her work. She wanted to change the law so that no one's freedom could ever be kept from them. It was a hard fight. Yet, Susan Anthony was determined to win.

She began to go from town to town to talk to people about freedom. She would talk with anyone who would listen. In the winter of 1854 Susan visited many towns. She walked from door to door, often in the biting cold. Sometimes people would listen to her. Sometimes doors were slammed in her face. Still, Susan went on. It was important work. It was work that only she could do.

Finally, after many long years, Susan's work helped bring many women more freedom. In 1860 the state of New York passed a law that gave married women the right to own property. It also allowed them to keep their earnings. It was an important moment. It was an exciting moment. It was a great victory for freedom. Susan B. Anthony had begun a movement for freedom that would soon sweep across our country.

Susan had the support of many important men and women. One of these was the famous black newspaper editor, Frederick Douglass. Another was Horace Greeley. They helped Susan B. Anthony in her great fight for freedom.

In 1868 Susan founded a weekly newspaper, called *The Revolution*. It was all about women's rights. The publishing office soon became a meeting place for leaders in the women's rights movement. It was a busy place. Many famous people wrote articles and stories to be printed in the paper.

Through *The Revolution* Susan B. Anthony became known all over the country for her bold stand on freedom. She wrote many articles which were printed in the paper. But she did many other things also. She sold advertising and took stories to the printer. She raised money. She even sold copies of the newspaper. However, she was not able to sell enough copies to pay the bills. In

At the ballot box. In 1872 Susan B. Anthony became the first woman in America to vote in a national election. She was arrested* and fined for this. Freedom was important to Susan B. Anthony. For more than sixty years she worked to help people understand that women should have the same rights and freedoms as men. Not everyone listened, at first. Yet, she worked to make freedom real for all Americans.

1870 Susan had to give up *The Revolution.* Sadly, she left its once busy offices to begin traveling again. She visited many states and cities with her powerful words of freedom. In 1871, for example, Susan spoke at 170 meetings, from New York to California.

In 1872 Susan Anthony took a bold step . . . a step that no woman had ever taken before. On November 5, she voted in the national election.* She encouraged other women to vote. By evening, fifteen other women had followed in her steps. Although she was arrested* for disobeying the voting laws, Susan Anthony had set a great movement in motion . . . a movement that would not stop . . . a movement that required great courage* and dedication to freedom. Finally, Congress passed a law giving women the right to vote. This was called woman suffrage. It gave to millions of Americans a freedom that had long been kept from them . . . a freedom that Susan B. Anthony knew one day would come.

• What are some of the ways in which Susan B. Anthony helped women gain more freedom?

Demanding rights for women. Susan B. Anthony set a great movement in motion. Women all over our country began to fight for the right to vote. In time, they succeeded. Today, women play an important part in electing government leaders.

Clara Barton started the American Red Cross in 1881. She devoted her life to helping others.

6 Clara Barton

Little Clara Barton tiptoed softly into her brother David's room. She gently felt his forehead to see if his fever had gone down. Then she filled a glass with cold water. Clara carefully measured out a teaspoon of medicine. Three months earlier, David had been badly hurt. He fell from

b. 1821

d. 1912

1700   1800   1900   2000

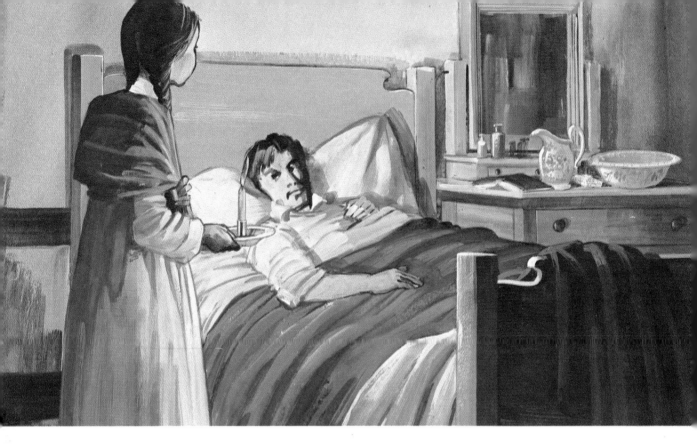

Loyalty

See Great Ideas

Clara Barton nursed her brother when he was badly hurt. While helping others she forgot her shyness. Throughout her life she put the needs of other people ahead of her own. Clara Barton helped wounded soldiers in wartime. She also helped the poor and the homeless in peacetime. Clara Barton's life gave meaning to the great idea of loyalty.

the roof of a barn. Since then, Clara had been his nurse.

Clara enjoyed helping other people. Perhaps this was one reason why everyone on the big Barton farm loved her. She was the favorite of all her older brothers and sisters. When she was only three, Sally and Dorothy taught her to read and spell. Before she was four, Stephen carried her on his shoulders to school. By the time she was five,

David was teaching her to ride horseback and to play ball well.

Home was the only place where Clara was really happy. This was because she was very shy. Galloping on a spirited horse did not frighten her. But she was terribly afraid of meeting new people. As she grew older, Clara learned that when she was helping other people she forgot about herself. Then she stopped being shy.

Clara decided to find some kind of work which would help other people. When she was fifteen, she began to teach school. She taught for eighteen years. Then her voice failed. She could no longer teach. After resting for a while, she went to work for our government in Washington, D.C.

While Clara was in Washington, the Civil War* broke out. Wounded soldiers came to the city from the battlefield. Clara and several other women helped to take care of these

*See Glossary

Clara Barton went to Washington, D.C., to work for our government. The Civil War soon broke out.

On the battlefield. Clara Barton risked her life many times to help wounded soldiers during the Civil War.* Later, she urged the Red Cross to help victims* of peacetime disasters as well.

soldiers' wounds. In a newspaper, Clara asked for food and clothing for these men. People sent so much that she had to rent a place in which to store these goods. Then she gave them to the soldiers.

Clara Barton's greatest work during this war was helping wounded soldiers on the battlefront. The army agreed to let her go to the places where the fighting was done. Forgetting about herself, she helped the sick and wounded. She comforted the dying. The grateful soldiers called her "The Angel of the Battlefield."

After the war, Clara went to Switzerland for a much-needed rest. While she was there, some gentlemen visited her. They told her about the Red Cross. The Red Cross had been formed to help all wounded soldiers. It did not matter what country they were fighting for. Before long, Clara

Clara Barton served as president* of the American Red Cross for more than twenty years. The Red Cross helps people in war and in peace. Clara Barton gave her life to helping people in need.

decided that the Red Cross should be started in America also.

Clara Barton remained in Europe for four years. During her stay, the German and French people fought each other in a bitter war. Clara helped the Red Cross workers in Europe care for the wounded soldiers. After the war, she helped in other ways. She helped give food, clothing, and money to people who were hungry and had no homes. Several European leaders honored her. They were grateful for her help.

Then Miss Barton returned to the United States. She worked hard to start the Red Cross in our country. In 1882, the American Red Cross joined the International Red Cross. Clara did not stop with this victory, however. She believed that the Red Cross should also help people during peacetime. It should help victims* of floods, bad storms, and epidemics.* Clara asked the American Red Cross to give this kind of help. Soon she was also able to get the International Red Cross to help in these ways, too.

Clara Barton served as president* of the American Red Cross for more than twenty years. She was a great American who forgot about herself in helping others.

- How did Clara Barton overcome her shyness?
- Why was Clara Barton called "The Angel of the Battlefield"?
- What were some of the ways Clara Barton served the people of our country?
- What important work did Clara Barton urge the Red Cross to do?
- When was the American Red Cross started?

Franklin Roosevelt was the only man ever elected* to serve four terms as president.*

7 Franklin and Eleanor Roosevelt

Franklin Delano Roosevelt stood before a huge crowd in Washington, D.C. He was about to make an inaugural* speech. Roosevelt had just been chosen president* of the United States. The year was 1933.

In millions of homes people moved closer to their radios. They wanted to hear what their new president had to say. Americans were frightened by a terrible depression.* One fourth of our workers had no jobs. Slowly,

President Roosevelt spoke to the American people. His words were strong. He brought new hope and courage* to the people of our country.

Young Franklin Roosevelt grew up at his father's beautiful home in Hyde Park, New York. As a boy he loved to swim and ice-skate. He also rode horses. In summer he often went on trips to Europe with his family. His family was very well

*See Glossary

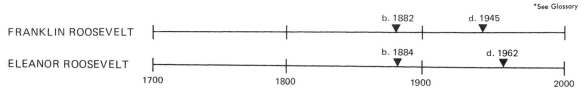

FRANKLIN ROOSEVELT — b. 1882 / d. 1945

ELEANOR ROOSEVELT — b. 1884 / d. 1962

1700   1800   1900   2000

known. His cousin, Theodore Roosevelt, was our twenty-sixth president.

After law school, Franklin worked as a lawyer for three years. In 1910, he decided that serving in the government would be more interesting and exciting. He ran for the New York Senate. In a bright red car he drove to almost every village in his district. He shook hands. He made speeches. And he made many friends. These friends voted for him. He was elected* to the state senate. Later, he was made Assistant Secretary of the Navy.

In August, 1921, his life was greatly changed. A sickness called polio* paralyzed the muscles in his legs. For many months he could not walk. This might have ended the public life of another man. But it did not end the public life of Franklin Roosevelt. During many years he never lost hope. He learned to walk with crutches. Later he was able to walk with heavy steel braces.

Then in 1928 Franklin was elected governor of the state of New York. His body was crippled. His spirit was strong. His courage gave millions of people hope. People believed in Franklin Roosevelt. Perhaps this is why he was elected president during the dark years of the depression.

Running for vice-president. In 1920 Franklin Roosevelt ran for vice-president. He was not elected. Later, he was elected to our country's highest office.

In 1933 millions of people were out of work. They had no money. Families lost their homes. Many factories had to close their doors. There were few jobs. Many people in ragged clothes sold apples on the streets. They hoped to earn money to buy food.

Franklin Roosevelt became president in March, 1933. With the help of his wife, Eleanor, he made many bold plans. He told people about them on the radio. These talks were called "fireside chats." Soon his plans were called the "New Deal." In time, things began to get better. During his years in office, many new laws were passed. Some of them made new jobs. Others gave money to people who could not work.

Eleanor was an able woman. She was also very warm and kind. She cared about people. Like her husband, she wanted to help people. In a way, she became Franklin's legs. She went across our country to talk with people. She listened to their troubles. She looked for ways to help them. At the White House she would tell Franklin what people thought and said. Often, people were surprised to get letters from the President and Eleanor. It made them feel that the President of the United States cared about their troubles.

Eleanor also helped people in other ways. She helped to start a camp for girls who had no families.

With our soldiers. During World War II* Eleanor Roosevelt went to many parts of the world to visit our soldiers. They were often surprised to see the President's wife in distant army camps.

A world at war. Franklin Roosevelt led the American people through a terrible war. He was a great leader. He gave people courage* and hope. Franklin Roosevelt helped to bring freedom to people in many countries. He was commander in chief of our armed forces during World War II. Franklin Roosevelt led the greatest fight for freedom the world has ever known.

She worked to find homes for people in need. Once, she sent her own doctor to see a family too poor to pay for a doctor's care. She was a kind person. Eleanor earned the love of people for the many things she did.

Eleanor also called meetings with newspaper people at the White House. A president's wife had never done this before. She talked with these people about things that needed to be done to make life better. She and Franklin worked hard to make his "New Deal" succeed.

Eleanor and Franklin also worked hard to help our country during World War II.* Franklin had to make many important choices. He worked with leaders of other friendly countries. Eleanor went all over the world to visit our soldiers. Many people were surprised to see the President's wife in army camps.

Franklin and Eleanor Roosevelt helped to bring America through some of its worst times. They guided us through the depression and a terrible war. They gave people new hope. People all over the world loved and looked up to the Roosevelts.

Franklin was the only president ever elected to four terms in office. Franklin and Eleanor Roosevelt were two of our great Americans.

- What great tragedy did Franklin Roosevelt overcome in his life?
- How did Franklin and Eleanor Roosevelt serve the people of our country?

Roosevelt and Churchill. During World War II, Franklin Roosevelt worked closely with Winston Churchill in a great struggle for freedom. Churchill was Prime Minister of England. Throughout this war the American and English peoples fought together to make the world free.

Henry Ford and his first automobile. In 1896 Ford built his first automobile. Soon he was building automobiles that many people could afford to buy.

8 Henry Ford

When Henry Ford was a small boy, he was interested in machines on his father's farm. His father hoped that Henry would become a farmer. However, the only thing about the farm that Henry liked was the machinery. He kept his father's machinery repaired. He also worked on the neighbors' clocks and farm machines when he had time.

When he was sixteen, Henry left the farm. He walked to the nearby city of Detroit, Michigan. His first job was as an apprentice* in a machine shop. Later, he worked in engine shops where he learned to build

*See Glossary

b. 1863   d. 1947

1700   1800   1900   2000

and repair steam engines. These jobs gave him the training he needed to begin experiments* on an automobile.

Many years passed before Henry Ford could spend all his time on experiments. He worked at different jobs to earn a living. At twenty-four, he left his job as a machine worker and ran a sawmill near his father's farm. Later, he returned to Detroit. He worked for the Edison Illuminating Company.

No matter what job Henry had, his real work went on at home. While working for the Edison Company in

Henry Ford built his first automobile in a workshop behind his home. Henry built the car by hand. He finished it in 1896. By 1925 Ford's factory produced a new car every fifteen seconds.
Photograph courtesy of the Ford Archives

Ford changed America. All over our country people sold their horses and bought automobiles. In a few years, Henry Ford's low-cost automobile changed the way that people traveled. People could travel farther in less time by automobile.

Detroit, he set up a workshop in a shed behind his house. Here, he built his first "horseless carriage."

Late one night in 1896 the little car was ready to run. But Ford discovered he couldn't get it out of the shed. The door was too small. This did not stop him for long. He cut a hole in the wall and drove his car right through it to the street.

Ford drove the car often after this first run. How everybody stared at the strange machine! It had a boxlike body, bicycle wheels, and a stick to steer with. People laughed when he got out and turned the car around by hand. The little car could not even go backward.

Henry Ford was not the first man to build a "horseless carriage." Cars

The first Ford plant. In this tiny building, Henry Ford started his assembly line. Within a few years, Ford had assembly lines in many parts of the world.

were already being sold in the United States and Europe. These cars were made by hand, and they cost a lot of money. Ford hoped to build cars at a low cost. Then, people with small incomes could buy them. Most people in business laughed at this idea. They thought the automobile would always be a "rich man's toy."

Ford proved them wrong. In 1903 he opened a small automobile factory. In twenty years he was building cars at a low cost. Many people could now buy them. Many thousands of each part were made in Ford's factory. The frames were placed on a moving belt that took them along a row of workers. As a frame came by, each worker put on a different part. When the cars reached the end of this "assembly line," they were ready to be driven

away. This method of building is called "mass production." By 1925, mass production made it possible for Ford's workers to build four cars a minute. After Ford proved that this method would work, other companies began to use it.

Henry Ford surprised the whole country in 1914. He said that ten million dollars of his company's

Division of Labor

See Great Ideas

An early Ford assembly line. Henry Ford invented* the assembly line. It is now used in factories all over the world. It changed the way people worked. Ford's assembly line allowed each person to work at a single job, rather than at many different jobs. This idea is called division of labor. It allows people to produce goods very quickly.

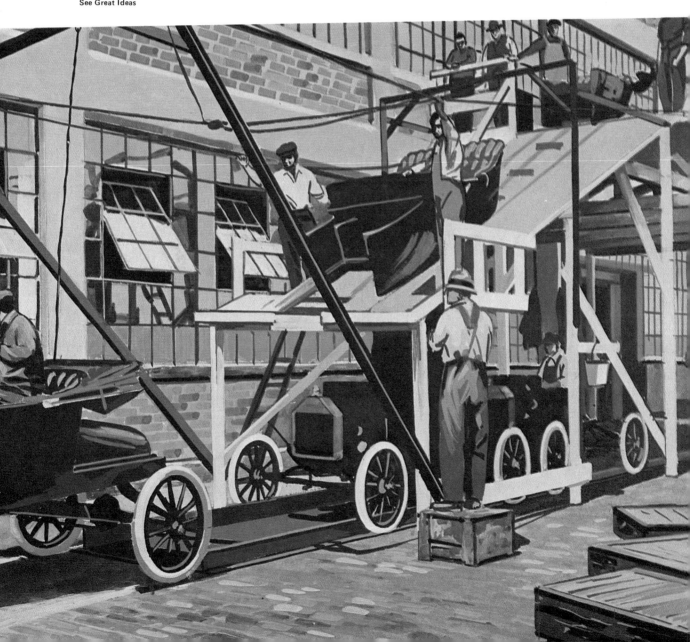

profits* were to be shared with his workers. At the same time he cut working hours. This had never been done before. Many people were sure his factory would now fail. The huge Ford plants all over the world show how wrong these people were.

- Where did Henry Ford build his first automobile?

- What idea did Henry Ford invent to help produce cars quickly?

- What form of transportation did Henry Ford's automobile help replace?

The Ford Plant at Dearborn, Michigan, is one of many Ford factories throughout the world. It is also one of the largest factories. Have you ever visited a factory like this?

Marching to Montgomery. Martin Luther and Coretta King helped lead a freedom march from Selma to Montgomery, Alabama. They marched to help black people gain many of the freedoms they had been denied. The National Guard was called out to protect the marchers.

9 Martin Luther King, Jr., and Coretta King

August 28 was a bright, clear day in Washington, D.C. Even in the hot sun, more than 200,000 people gathered peacefully in our country's capital. They had come to hear the stirring words of a young black minister* from Atlanta. The city was alive with excitement. The people

*See Glossary

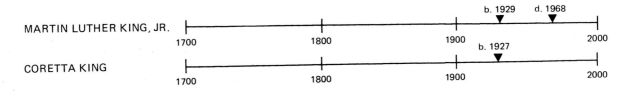

MARTIN LUTHER KING, JR.

| | 1700 | 1800 | 1900 | b. 1929 ▼ | d. 1968 ▼ | 2000 |

CORETTA KING

| | 1700 | 1800 | 1900 | b. 1927 ▼ | 2000 |

Freedom

See Great Ideas

"I have a dream." In 1963 Martin Luther King, Jr., and others led a great march in Washington, D.C. It was a march for freedom. More than 200,000 people gathered to hear Martin Luther King's stirring speech. Later, Dr. King met with President John F. Kennedy in the White House to talk about freedom. Martin Luther King devoted his life to helping people gain more freedom. He was put in jail. His home was bombed.* Yet, Martin Luther King did not stop. He believed in freedom. In 1968 he died for freedom.

came from all over America. They came from all walks of life. They came in old cars and crowded buses. Some came in long, shiny black automobiles. Many had walked to Washington, D.C., from faraway places. By noon the great crowd stretched from the Lincoln Memorial to the Washington Monument. Everywhere there were people, almost as far as you could see.

It was an exciting moment. As the young minister stood to speak, thundering waves of applause rose from the crowd. Then, as if by magic, over 200,000 voices began to chant his name.

"Martin Luther King," the voices chanted, louder and louder. "Martin Luther King."

August 28, 1963, was a great day for freedom. It was a great day for the young minister. Dr. Martin Luther King, Jr., and his lovely wife Coretta had come to share their dream for America . . . an America free of injustice . . . an America free of racial prejudice* . . . an America filled with the spirit of brotherhood. It was a great dream.

Millions of Americans listened to Dr. King's words on radio and television. Even the president* of our country listened carefully to Dr. King's powerful speech. Martin Luther King was the voice of freedom to people the world over. Only ten years earlier Martin Luther King was almost unknown outside Atlanta.

As a boy, Martin loved to listen to the sermons of his father, the Reverend Martin Luther King, Sr. From the age of six, young Martin was very active in his father's church. When he sang hymns, Martin often moved people to tears. He was bright and kind. People loved to be around him.

Some of Martin's playmates were white children who lived near the King home. One day Martin rushed home in tears. The parents of some of his white friends told him he could no longer play with the white children. At that time many white people believed that blacks were in-ferior.* Even though America was a free country, blacks were refused many freedoms simply because of the color of their skin. This was one of Martin's first experiences with prejudice. It hurt him so deeply that he never forgot it.

Such early experiences shaped Martin's plans. He wanted to help improve life for blacks in America. He wanted to fight for freedom and equal rights for all Americans.

While attending Morehouse College in Atlanta, Martin decided to become a minister. At eighteen, he became assistant minister of the Ebenezer Baptist Church. This was his father's church. He was so well known around Atlanta that people came from miles around to hear his first sermon. He was a powerful speaker. He made them think. Whenever Martin spoke, people wanted to shout with enthusiasm for what he was saying. They often did.

While attending Boston University, Martin met a music student named Coretta Scott. In a short time Martin and Coretta were married. The next year, 1954, they moved to Montgomery, Alabama. Martin was named the minister of the Dexter Avenue Baptist Church. This was where Martin and Coretta

In jail for freedom. Martin Luther King went to jail for his belief that all people should have equal rights.

On December 1, 1955, Mrs. Rosa Parks, a black woman, was arrested* by the Montgomery police. She had boarded a bus and refused to move to the back where blacks had to sit. Then she refused to give her seat to a white man.

When news of this reached Dr. King, he and other black leaders met. They decided to demonstrate* against the arrest of Rosa Parks. Dr. King was asked to lead the blacks. He agreed. However, he asked the people to demonstrate peacefully. They followed his wishes.

King began their great work for freedom.

At that time hatred of blacks was very strong in Montgomery and in other cities. Blacks were not allowed to sit with whites in eating places or on buses. Blacks were not allowed in many hotels and public places such as parks and swimming pools. Black children were not allowed to attend the same schools that white children attended. This was called segregation. Blacks were often treated badly. Sometimes they were beaten or killed.

This was the beginning of a great freedom movement in America. Over the next few years Dr. King led demonstrations and gave speeches in cities throughout our country. With the help of Coretta, Dr. King inspired thousands of people to stand up against hatred and injustice.

Dr. King was arrested many times. He spent many long, lonely nights in jail for his beliefs. This was very hard for Coretta. Yet, she helped him in every way possible. Sometimes she spoke to groups of people when Dr. King could not do so.

Dr. King's strong beliefs led him into danger many times. He led many peace marches in cities where hatred of blacks was strong. He sometimes faced long lines of police. He was kicked and beaten. Vicious dogs were turned loose on his followers. Once his home was even bombed.* But Dr. King refused to fight violence* with violence. He believed it was more courageous* to fight for justice with words. He knew the truth was more powerful than guns or clubs.

Soon after a great demonstration in Birmingham, Alabama, Dr. King's freedom movement quickly spread to cities in all parts of our country. He gave people hope that freedom and justice for all was possible.

Dr. King visited many cities. He traveled day after day to encourage people to demonstrate peacefully. In one year Dr. King gave 208 speeches and traveled 780,000 miles. Sometimes he became angry when he saw violence. He would not accept violence in his freedom movement.

After years of working for freedom, Dr. King received the Nobel

With King Olav of Norway. In 1964 Martin Luther King received the Nobel Peace Prize.* He received it for his great freedom work. Martin Luther King traveled thousands of miles and gave hundreds of speeches to help people gain more freedom.

Peace Prize*in 1964. His love for people and his dedication to freedom inspired the whole world. Even presidents and kings asked his advice. The young minister from Atlanta now belonged to the world. His interest in other people made him one of the most loved leaders of our country.

On April 4, 1968, a great tragedy* happened. Dr. Martin Luther King, Jr., was murdered as he stood on a motel balcony in Memphis, Tennessee. His life was cut short, but his great words live on. Today, Coretta King carries on the work she and her husband began together. Martin Luther and Coretta King gave the world the gift of hope . . . hope that people of every color will one day live together with freedom and dignity.

- What was the name of Martin Luther King's church?
- What great prize did Martin Luther King receive?
- Why do you think Martin Luther King spent his life helping others gain more freedom? Explain.

Loyalty

See Great Ideas

Coretta King has devoted much of her life to helping Martin Luther King work for freedom. Since her husband's death, she has continued this important work. Coretta King's life is an example of the great idea of loyalty to people.

Jonas Salk in his Pittsburgh laboratory. Salk worked for four years to develop the Salk vaccine.*

10 Jonas Salk

It was a hot summer day in 1952. Polio* season had begun. All over the country families waited in fear for the terrible illness to strike without warning. Ambulances lined up at hospitals with hundreds of new polio cases each day. Hospital beds and hallways were crowded with thousands of new victims.* Most polio victims were children.

For four years Dr. Jonas Salk worked tirelessly in his Pittsburgh laboratory. He was searching for a way to end the horror of polio. Many times Dr. Salk walked the halls of Municipal Hospital in his

*See Glossary

b. 1914

1700   1800   1900   2000

long white coat. He was trying to comfort children sick with polio. Their cries of pain often brought tears to his soft, kindly eyes.

Dr. Salk worked day and night on his experiments,* often meeting failure at every turn. Time after time his assistants were ready to give up. Dr. Salk inspired them to go on with their important work. His quiet strength and friendly smile encouraged them. How could he even think of giving up when children were dying only yards away from his laboratory?

On July 2, 1952, Dr. Salk drove over dusty, country roads to the small town of Leetsdale. He was going to conduct a secret experiment. Dr. Salk drove faster than usual. He had developed a new vaccine* that he believed would work against polio. He was eager to test it for the first time on people.

Inside the cool auditorium of the Watson Home for Crippled Children, Dr. Salk sat near the end of a long table. On the table were hypodermic* needles and cotton. The air was filled with the whispers and excited laughter of the children who lived at the home. It was an important day. They were going to help Dr. Salk with an important experiment.

Many of the children sat in wheelchairs or walked with crutches.

"Hi, Dr. Jonas," shouted a small, dark-haired boy in a wheelchair. Dr. Salk looked up and smiled broadly. He waved to his young friend.

One by one Dr. Salk inoculated* each child with his new vaccine. He was very gentle. Few of the children even felt the tiny needle prick their skin. As he worked, Dr. Salk laughed and talked with the children. They all knew and loved Dr. Salk. He was their friend. They knew he wanted to save other children from suffering. Everyone trusted Dr. Salk. He was that kind of person.

Bending over his microscope* late at night, Dr. Salk studied a tiny blood sample taken from one of the children at Leetsdale. What he saw excited him very much. The vaccine worked. He was sure it would prevent polio. Within a few years, millions of children were inoculated with the Salk vaccine. Polio was no longer something to fear, thanks to the courage* and dedication of Dr. Jonas Salk, our most loved medical scientist.*

Jonas Salk was the kind of boy you would expect to discover great things. Young Jonas was deeply interested in the world around him.

Immunizing* against polio.* Before Jonas Salk developed the Salk vaccine,* thousands of people died of polio. Today, few new cases are reported. Have you been immunized against polio?

He had a quick mind. He loved to read and to ask questions. He always wanted to know the "why" of things.

Jonas also had a great love for people. He felt compassion and tenderness for the suffering. He saw much suffering in the neighborhoods of

Education

See Great Ideas

The war against polio. Jonas Salk studied for many years to become a doctor. His polio research* took many more years. Education was important to Jonas Salk. It helped him save many lives. Without education Jonas Salk could never have developed the Salk vaccine. How important will education be to you?

New York City where he lived. Jonas wanted to be able to help people someday.

At New York's City College, Jonas discovered the world of science. He loved to conduct experiments and would spend hours over his microscope.

In college Jonas decided to become a doctor. He wanted to discover new things, things that would help people and make a better world.

At the New York University School of Medicine, Jonas spent as much time as he could in the laboratory. He wanted to learn everything about the causes of disease. His teachers liked Jonas. He studied very hard and sometimes worked in the laboratory long after everyone else had gone home. Jonas eventually decided not to treat patients. Instead, he wanted to give his life to research.* He wanted to help discover causes of sickness.

In 1948 Jonas Salk began his research on polio with a team of assistants while at Pittsburgh's Municipal Hospital. At that time there was no way to keep people from becoming sick with polio. Doctors were helpless against it.

Some medical scientists believed that no vaccine could ever work against polio. Others believed that a vaccine of live polio viruses* might be made to prevent polio. This was very dangerous. It would mean giving people the polio virus in the hope that they would develop an immunity* to the disease.

Dr. Salk questioned the accepted ideas of the medical scientists. He believed that it might be possible to make a vaccine from dead polio viruses that would be both safe and effective against polio. Many scientists laughed at this, but Dr. Salk believed in himself and in his idea.

Soon Dr. Salk set up his own laboratory in Pittsburgh to test his idea and to carry out research. He and his assistants tried hundreds of different combinations of drugs. They tested them on thousands of monkeys. Dr. Salk gave much of his life to the fight against polio. He sometimes worked seven days a week, and even twenty-four hours at a time, without rest. His weary assistants worked equally hard. They were inspired by Dr. Salk's selfless work.

Dr. Salk worked carefully on his research, and often tried experiments again and again to be sure his findings were correct. He had faith in himself and in his new vaccine.

Dr. Salk wanted nothing for himself. He did not care about money. He cared only about people, people in need. He gave his vaccine freely to the world. No one would ever again needlessly suffer the horrors of polio. Today Dr. Jonas Salk is loved by people all over the world for his gift of the Salk vaccine.

- How did Jonas Salk help people?
- How did education help Jonas Salk succeed?

Salk with President Jimmy Carter. In 1977 Jonas Salk received the Medal of Freedom* at the White House. This is one of the greatest honors that an American can receive. Why do you think Jonas Salk deserved the Medal of Freedom?

First person on the moon. As a boy, Neil Armstrong had a great dream. He wanted to fly.

11   Neil A. Armstrong

Neil Armstrong always wanted to fly. It was his great dream. He took his first airplane ride at the age of six. It was exciting to soar high among the clouds. This was in 1936. He never forgot that day. From that time on Neil Armstrong dreamed of one day learning to fly.

While other boys played football or baseball, Neil had more important things to do. He was much too busy for games. He loved to build model airplanes. He also read many books and magazines about flying. You could almost say that flying was his whole life, even then.

b. 1930

1700   1800   1900   2000

Neil was a very bright boy. He was very hardworking. When he was old enough, he got a job after school. He wanted to earn money to pay for flying lessons. He worked as a clerk in hardware and drug stores. At that time, flying lessons cost nine dollars an hour. He only earned forty cents an hour. Many boys would have given up, but not Neil Armstrong. He worked hard and saved his money. He was going to learn to fly. He was going to be a pilot.

Neil worked hard toward his goal. He started flying lessons at fourteen. When he was sixteen he passed his flying test. He was an airplane pilot, at last. Other boys his age were just learning to drive cars. Neil Armstrong could fly among the clouds.

He went through high school in his hometown of Wapakoneta, Ohio. He later went to Purdue University. In 1949 he became a fighter pilot for the United States Navy. This was during the Korean War.* In three years he flew nearly eighty combat flights in Korea. Once his jet was shot down behind enemy lines. Another time he flew a damaged plane to a safe landing on an aircraft carrier.

Neil Armstrong was a good pilot . . . so good that he was asked to become a test pilot after he left the navy. As a test pilot, Neil flew many different kinds of airplanes. Most of them had never been flown before. It was his job to make sure they were safe to fly. Other pilots' lives depended on him. He was the kind of man you could always depend on.

One of the airplanes he flew was the X-15. It was a very special airplane. It was part airplane and part rocket. In the X-15 he sometimes flew 4,000 miles an hour. He went as high as thirty-eight miles. No other airplane had flown as fast or as high as the X-15. It was a dangerous job. One mistake could mean instant death. Neil Armstrong flew the X-15 without any accidents.

In 1962 he became an astronaut. This was at the beginning of our country's space program. It was hard to become an astronaut. Many people tried. Only the very best were selected. Astronaut training was also hard. There was much to learn about space and space flight. Many tests were made to see if the astronauts could live in space. Most important of all was courage.* An astronaut's job is dangerous . . . perhaps the most dangerous job in the world. Neil Armstrong trained for four years to become an astronaut.

*See Glossary

Going to the moon. Neil Armstrong leads the astronauts to the Apollo 11 spacecraft. It was the morning of July 16, 1969. Four days later Neil Armstrong took his first step on the moon.

In 1966 he was launched into space for the first time. His spacecraft was called Gemini 8. He and another astronaut, David Scott, were going to try something new. They were going to connect Gemini 8 with another spacecraft. During the test something went wrong. Gemini 8 began to roll out of control. Quickly, the astronauts changed course. They flew back to Earth and landed safely in the ocean. Both men could have been killed in space. Neil Armstrong's quick thinking had saved them.

In 1969 Neil began preparing for a great adventure ... the greatest adventure of his life. He and another astronaut were going to land on the moon. This had never been done before. Many people believed it would be impossible. It would be the most dangerous space flight ever made. And it would be the most exciting.

The moon is more than 240,000 miles from Earth. To get there the astronauts had to depend on the work of thousands of people. Some built the rockets. Others tested them. Still others worked in the control center. The rockets had more than a million parts. This meant that any one of a million things could go wrong.

On July 16, 1969, Apollo 11 was launched at Cape Canaveral.*Aboard were Michael Collins, Edwin Aldrin, and Neil Armstrong. Neil Armstrong was chosen to be the first person to walk on the moon. Apollo 11 traveled at a speed of nearly 25,000 miles an hour. The trip to the moon took three days. On the following day, July 20, people would land on the moon for the first time.

The moon landing craft was called the Eagle. Inside it were Aldrin and Armstrong. The Eagle was connected to the spaceship. This was the Columbia. When the Eagle separated from the Columbia, Neil Armstrong radioed, "The Eagle has wings."

Blasting off. Powerful rockets sent Apollo 11 rushing into space at a speed of nearly 25,000 miles per hour. The trip to the moon made by Apollo 11 took three days.

Soon the astronauts got close to the moon. It was time to land. But something was wrong. Neil saw that the moon's surface was covered with large rocks. His heart began to beat faster. If they tried to land there the Eagle would crash. There were only seconds left. He knew something had to be done quickly. The success of Apollo 11 depended on him. With quick thinking he took over the controls. He searched for a clear place to land. Skillfully he landed the Eagle. It settled gently on the moon. Huge clouds of moon dust rose from the surface. At last, people had landed on the moon.

To millions of people Neil Armstrong radioed back a quiet, simple message.

"Tranquility base here. The Eagle has landed," he said. His words were heard on televisions and radios all over the world.

Several hours later, Neil Armstrong climbed slowly down the Eagle's ladder and set foot on the moon. The moon was silent and empty.

As he stepped on the moon, he said, "That's one small step for a man, one giant leap for mankind." It was a great moment. The impossible was now possible. At last, people had

Mirror on the moon. Neil Armstrong's image is seen in Edwin Aldrin's space helmet. Armstrong was the first person to walk on the moon. He proved the impossible is sometimes possible.

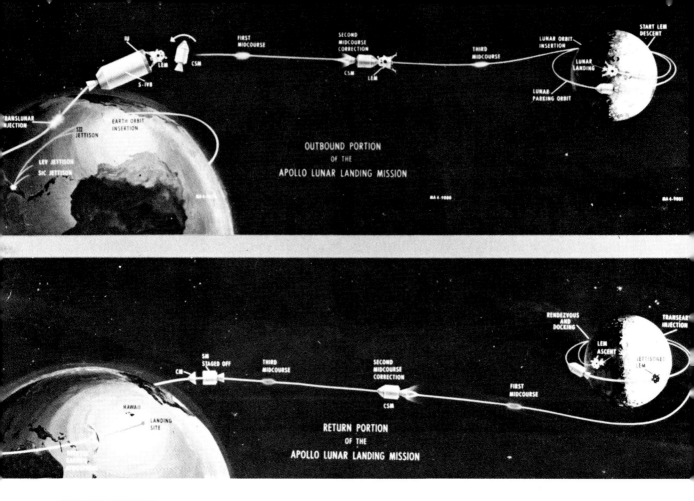

OUTBOUND PORTION
OF THE
APOLLO LUNAR LANDING MISSION

RETURN PORTION
OF THE
APOLLO LUNAR LANDING MISSION

Cooperation

See Great Ideas

The top picture shows the trip to the moon. The bottom picture shows Apollo 11's return to the earth. The first landing on the moon would not have happened without the cooperation of many thousands of people. Some helped to make the rockets. Some helped to make the spaceship. Other people planned the trip. Still others worked in the control center, making sure everything went smoothly. Without the hard work of many people, Neil Armstrong would never have walked on the moon. In what ways is cooperation important in your life? In what ways do you need the cooperation of your family?

reached the distant moon. They had walked on it. And Neil Armstrong, the boy who always wanted to fly, was the first one there.

- Why was cooperation important to the success of Apollo 11?

- What did Neil Armstrong say when he first stepped on the moon? What did his words mean?

HERE MEN FROM THE PLANET EARTH
FIRST SET FOOT UPON THE MOON
JULY 1969, A. D.
WE CAME IN PEACE FOR ALL MANKIND

NEIL A. ARMSTRONG
ASTRONAUT

MICHAEL COLLINS
ASTRONAUT

EDWIN E. ALDRIN, JR.
ASTRONAUT

RICHARD NIXON
PRESIDENT, UNITED STATES OF AMERICA

Index

Acknowledgments

Grateful acknowledgment is made to the following for permission to use the illustrations found in this book:

Alpha Photo Associates: Page 13
American Heritage: Page 9; page 7 with permission of Washington & Lee University
Beerhorst: Page 8
Country Beautiful: Page 1, painting by David Martin. With permission from the Washington Historical Society
Ford Motor Company: Pages 41 and 46
Fraunces Tavern Museum, Sons of the Revolution in the State of New York: Pages 10-11, painting by John Ward Dunsmore
Freelance Photographers Guild; Pages 30 and 36; page 52 by Fletcher Drake
Harry Abrams, Inc.: Pages 2-3 with permission of Norman Rockwell
Historical Pictures Service: Pages 23, 44, and 56; page 21, painting by Henry H. Cross
Johnson Publishing Company: Pages 47, 48, and 50
NASA: Pages 59, 61, 62, 63, and 64 (both)
Painting by J. N. Marchand: Pages 24-25

Photoreporters: Page 51
Rinehart-Marsden, Inc.: Page 15
Silver Burdett: Page 31
The American Red Cross: Page 33 (top) by Matthew Brady
The Bettmann Archive: Pages 27 and 53
The Fideler Company: Pages 4-5, 6, 14, 16-17, 32, 33 (bottom), 34-35, and 44-45; pages 26 and 29, paintings by Diane Bartnick
The Ford Archives: Page 42; page 43, painting by Norman Rockwell
The Franklin D. Roosevelt Library: Page 40
The National Foundation of the March of Dimes: Page 55
The Smithsonian Institute: Page 19
The Virginia Museum of Fine Arts: Page 12, painting by J. B. Stearns
The White House: Page 58
United Press International: Page 37
Wide World Photos: Page 39; page 38 courtesy of Franklin D. Roosevelt Library

GREAT IDEAS

The Lincoln Memorial, in Washington, D.C. Abraham Lincoln was our sixteenth president. He believed in the great idea of freedom for all citizens.

People using computers* in a business office. A computer is a machine that stores information, much as people store facts in their minds. The computer uses this information to solve difficult problems. Would you say that a computer is a kind of tool? Explain. Make a list of different tools used by people in our country. Could Americans meet their needs without using any of these tools? Give facts to back up your answer.

*See Glossary

Great Ideas

People have been living in America for thousands of years. During this time, they have always lived in communities.* No person can meet his or her needs all alone. (See "Our Needs" on pages 130-131.) Only by living and working with other people can a person have a happy life.

In order to make community life successful, people have followed certain ways of living. We call these the "great ideas."

These great ideas have played an important part in our country's history. They still affect the lives of Americans today. Ten of these great ideas are:

1. Freedom
2. Rules and government
3. Cooperation
4. Loyalty
5. Language
6. Education
7. Using natural resources
8. Using tools
9. Division of labor
10. Exchange

The following chapters give valuable information about these great ideas. Read each chapter carefully. As you read, try to discover how each great idea has helped build our nation.

1 Freedom

■ What is freedom?

No idea is more important to Americans than the idea of freedom. Our national song, "The Star-Spangled Banner," calls the United States "the land of the free." All of our coins have the word "liberty" on them. Liberty is another word for freedom. The Statue of Liberty in New York City is a famous symbol* of our country. So is the Liberty Bell in Philadelphia.

Freedom in American history. Freedom has played an important part in our history. Long ago, many tribes of Indians lived in North America. These people had a great deal of freedom to live as they pleased. In the 1600's, settlers began coming to America from Europe. Many came because they did not have enough freedom at home. They hoped to find more freedom in America.

Two hundred years ago, the American settlers went to war against Great Britain. Their goal was to gain more freedom. The Americans started a new nation, called the United States. This nation was based on the idea of freedom for all people.

Freedom and responsibility.* What do we mean by the word "freedom"? People are said to be free if they can do as they please without being controlled by anyone else. Of course, no one is ever completely free. Some people have a large amount of freedom. Others have hardly any freedom at all.

When people have freedom, they also have responsibilities. In other words, there are certain things they must do to protect their freedom. For example, they must obey the laws of their community. Also, they must be willing to do some kind of useful work. If people do not meet their responsibilities, they will not have freedom for very long.

*See Glossary

The President of the United States speaking to a group of labor* union members in California. In the United States, most people enjoy a large amount of freedom. What kinds of freedom are shown in this picture? You may want to read the rest of the chapter before answering this question.

Kinds of freedom. There are several different kinds of freedom. Three kinds of freedom have been especially important in building our nation. These are:

1. Political* freedoms
2. Religious freedom
3. Economic* freedom

In the following pages, you will learn more about these different kinds of freedom. You will discover how each kind of freedom has helped to shape our nation's history.

- Do you think people everywhere in the world have a strong desire for freedom? Why? Why not?
- How important is freedom to you? What things would you be willing to give up in order to have freedom?
- Do laws take away people's freedom to do certain things? Are there times when laws help to protect people's freedom? Explain.

Political Freedoms

■ What are political freedoms, and why are they important?

Our country, the United States, is a democracy. This means that the citizens have a share in the government. (See page 27.) They can help choose the people who make and carry out the laws.

It would not be possible to have a democracy without certain kinds of freedom. These are known as political freedoms. Four of the most important political freedoms are:

1. Freedom of speech.

A candidate* for a government office speaking to voters in the early 1800's. Would it be possible to have a government like ours without freedom of speech? Explain your answer.

2. Freedom of the press.

3. Freedom to assemble, or meet, with other people.

4. Freedom to send petitions* to government leaders.

What if our citizens did not have these freedoms? They would find it hard to get information about the government. Without this informa-

tion, they could not vote wisely. They might choose leaders who could not do their jobs properly. Also, people would have no way to tell their leaders what ought to be done.

The Bill of Rights. Political freedoms have been important to Americans ever since our country was started. In 1791, ten amendments* were added to our Constitution.* Together, these amendments are known as the Bill of Rights. They list certain rights that the government may not take away from any citizen. Among these are the four political freedoms. Let us examine each of these freedoms more closely.

Freedom of speech. In America, people are free to say what they think about any subject. This is true even if their ideas are disliked by a majority* of people. Americans can criticize their leaders without fear of being punished. They can also suggest changes in the government.

Freedom of the press. Americans can also express their ideas in print —that is, in books, magazines, and newspapers. This is called freedom of the press. It goes back to colonial days. In 1734, a brave newspaper editor, John Peter Zenger, lived in New York City. He printed stories that criticized the royal governor of

New York. Zenger was thrown into prison. But a jury decided that he was not guilty of any crime. He was allowed to go free. Today, Americans do not need to worry about displeasing their government leaders. They can print almost anything they like.

Freedom of assembly. Another important kind of freedom in our country is freedom of assembly. People are free to meet together for any reason. They can start clubs. They can hold parades and public meetings. However, they must do these things in a peaceful, orderly way.

Two young men having an argument. They are attending a meeting in our nation's capital, Washington, D.C. What important kinds of freedom are shown in this picture? Can people disagree with one another and still work together for the good of the community? Explain.

A citizen presenting a petition* to the mayor of her city. What is a petition? Is it important for citizens to be able to send petitions to government leaders? Why? Why not?

Freedom of petition. In the United States, people are free to send petitions to government leaders. In their petitions, they can complain about things they believe are wrong. They can also suggest changes that ought to be made.

Our responsibilities. Whenever people have rights, they also have responsibilities. This is true of the four political freedoms. For example, you have freedom of speech.

But you do not have the right to tell lies about other people. You have the right to meet in a group. But you should not break the laws. Nor should you do anything that would take away the rights of other people.

- Of the four freedoms described here, which do you think is the most important? Why?

- Suppose you did not have any political freedoms. How would your life be different from what it is today?

Roman Catholic* settlers started the colony of Maryland in 1634. Why were the Catholics not allowed to worship as they pleased in England? Why did they think they would have more freedom in America? What other groups of people came to America in search of religious freedom?

Religious Freedom

■ **What groups of people came to America to gain religious freedom?**

In the United States, people worship God in many different ways. Some people are Roman Catholics.* Others belong to Protestant* churches, such as the Methodists and the Baptists. Still others are Jews,* Moslems,* Buddhists,* or Hindus.* In addition, there are millions of Americans who do not follow any religion at all. In our country, people of all different faiths live side by side in friendship.

A lack of religious freedom. In Europe during the 1600's, there was little religious freedom. At that time, there were often wars between people of different faiths. Most countries had an official church, to which the ruler belonged. All people were expected to belong to the same church as their ruler. If they did not, they could be punished severely.

The Puritans. In England, there was an official church headed by the king. It was called the Church of England. Many English people were not happy with this church. They wanted to make it more "pure" by changing it in certain ways. These people were called Puritans. A few Puritans wanted to break away from the Church of England entirely. They were known as Separatists.

The English king did not like to have people belong to other churches. The Separatists were not allowed to hold their own worship services. Sometimes they were put in jail. Finally a group of Separatists—the Pilgrims—decided to move to America. In that far-off land, they would be free to worship God as they chose.

In 1620, the Pilgrims came to America aboard the ship "Mayflower." They settled in what is now Massachusetts. There they started a colony called Plymouth. Later, other groups of Puritans came to America in search of religious freedom. They started settlements all over New England.*

Other settlers. The hope of religious freedom brought many other people to America. For example, Maryland was started by Roman Catholics. These people had not been allowed to worship freely in England. The Quakers,* too, had been treated badly because of their beliefs. They started the colony of Pennsylvania.

Puritan laws. The settlers in America wanted religious freedom for themselves. But they were not always willing to give this same freedom to others. For example, in Massachusetts the Puritans ran the government. All citizens had to pay taxes to support the Puritan church. They also had to obey the strict laws made by the Puritan leaders. Some people had beliefs that were different from those of the Puritans. But they did not dare to speak about their beliefs openly. If they did, they might be whipped, or punished in other ways.

Roger Williams. Some people felt it was wrong to force everyone to worship in a certain way. Among these people was a Puritan minister named Roger Williams. He left Massachusetts in 1636 and started the colony of Rhode Island. In Rhode Island, there were no laws favoring one religion over another. All people were free to worship God in any way they pleased.

The First Amendment. As time passed, many Americans came to feel the same way Roger Williams did. In 1791, the First Amendment was added to our Constitution. (See

Jewish boys lighting candles to celebrate Hanukkah. Why is this holiday a good time to think about religious freedom? If you do not know, read about Hanukkah in other books.

A Protestant* church service. Suppose that nearly all the people in our country were Protestants. Would they have the right to tell other Americans how they ought to worship? Explain.

page 7.) This amendment says the government must not interfere in any way with freedom of religion.

Today, people in the United States have a great deal of religious freedom. There is no official church that everyone has to attend or pay taxes to support. Americans can worship God in any way they please. At the same time, they must not do any-thing to take the same freedom away from other people.

- The American settlers had more religious freedom than people in England. What do you think were the reasons for this?

- What if there was no freedom of religion in the United States? Do you think your life would be any different? Why? Why not?

A peddler in New England. In the 1800's, many peddlers traveled around our country. They sold goods to people who lived on farms. Do you think these peddlers had very much economic* freedom? Explain. Why do you suppose there are few peddlers in the United States today?

Economic Freedom

■ How do Americans use their economic freedom?

"What kind of work are you going to do when you grow up?" Young people in our country are often asked this question by friends or relatives.

Earning a living in Europe. In Europe several hundred years ago, there was no need to ask this question. Most people were not free to decide for themselves how they wanted to earn their living. Instead, they were expected to do the same kind of work as their parents. Many farmers in Europe were almost like slaves. These people were called serfs. All their lives, they had to work for rich landowners. It did not matter how much a serf disliked his work. He could not leave it and get a different job.

Earning a living in America. The settlers who came to America had much more economic freedom. In America, they could get land free or at a very low cost. They could start farms and work for themselves.

If they did not like farming, they could work at other jobs. In America, there was a great need for all kinds of workers. Suppose a man did not like his job. He could easily quit and find another one that suited him better.

Even in America, not everyone had economic freedom. Women were not free to do any kind of work they chose. They were expected to stay at home and do housework. Most black people in America were slaves. They had to work all their lives for white masters.

Economic freedom today. Today, most Americans enjoy a large amount of economic freedom. They can choose the kind of work they want to do. If they do not like their work, they can quit and get a different job. They can join labor* unions.

A student learning to work with metal in a shop class. Do you think economic freedom helps people to make good use of their talents? Explain your answer.

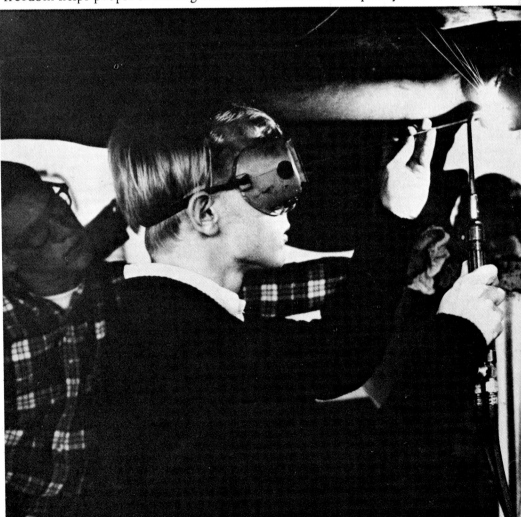

Through these groups, they can try to get higher pay and other benefits. Americans can own land and other kinds of property.* They can start businesses of their own. They are free to run these businesses as they please. However, they must be careful not to break any laws or cause harm to other people.

In America, people can decide for themselves how to spend the money they earn. They must use some of this money to pay taxes. But they can spend the rest on things they want for themselves. In America, many kinds of goods are available at prices most people can afford to pay.

- How would you explain economic freedom in your own words?

- Suppose you lived in a country where there was little economic freedom. What do you think your life would be like?

- Do you think women in our country have as much economic freedom as men do? Explain your answer.

Cesar Chavez (in the center of the picture below) was born in Arizona of Mexican parents. He started a labor union to help farm workers get higher pay and better working conditions. What are unions? How do they work? Look in other books to find answers to these questions.

Smokey the Bear has an important message for people who visit our nation's forests. Are there certain rules that you should follow in order to prevent forest fires? If so, what are they?

2 Rules and Government

■ How do rules help to make life safer and more pleasant?

One of the best-known cartoon characters in the United States is Smokey the Bear. For years, Smokey has been appearing on signs and posters of the United States Forest Service. Smokey's message is: be careful when you go into the woods so that you do not cause a forest fire.

A **forest fire** may destroy millions of trees. How do you suppose this fire started? Do you think it might have been prevented if people had followed certain rules? Explain your answer.

Smokey asks people who visit our country's forests to follow certain rules. For example:

. . . Never throw a lighted match or a burning cigarette on the ground.

. . . If you build a campfire, make sure it is in a place where it cannot spread to nearby trees.

. . . Never leave a campfire burning without someone to watch over it.

Let's think about what may happen if these rules are not followed. Imagine that a careless person drops a lighted match into a pile of dry leaves. The leaves begin to burn. The flames spread to trees and bushes nearby. Soon the whole forest is on fire. The roaring of the flames can be heard miles away. A great cloud of black smoke fills the sky. When

the fire is finally over, the beautiful tall trees are gone. In their place are dead, black stumps. Many years will pass before new trees grow up to replace the ones that were destroyed.

Every year, forest fires destroy millions of trees in our nation's forests. Most of these fires were started by people who failed to obey the rules of fire safety.

- Why do you suppose some persons do not follow the rules for preventing forest fires?
- What are some other ways in which people can cause great harm to themselves or to other people by not following the rules?

After the fire. What feelings do you have when you look at this picture? Do you think there should be some kind of punishment for people who cause forest fires by not obeying the rules? Explain.

■ How do people use rules in their everyday lives?

Whenever people live in groups, they need to follow certain rules in order to get along with one another. This is true even in families. If all the members of a family had exactly the same wishes and goals, there would be no need for rules. But this never happens in real life. Every member of a family has certain wishes and goals that are somewhat different from those of other persons in the family. Rules are needed to prevent arguments. They give each person in the family a chance to meet his or her needs.

If people could never agree on any rules to follow, life would be very different. People could not even play any games, because there are no games without rules. They would not be able to trust each other. They could not work together to reach

A friendly game of checkers. What are some of the rules that people must follow in order to play checkers? Are there any games that can be played without rules? Explain your answer.

Looking at the plans for a new house. Are there certain rules that the members of this family need to follow in order to get along with one another? If so, what are some of these rules?

important goals. Most people would not feel very safe. They probably would not be happy.

- What are some of the rules that you have to follow at home? Do you agree with all of these rules? Explain. What do you think it would be like to live in a family where there were no rules?

- What rules do you have to follow in your school? Why do you suppose these rules are needed? Are students more likely to reach their goals in school if they follow the rules? Explain.

- What happens when people break the rules? Are they hurting themselves? Are they hurting others? Explain.

■ Who makes the rules for a community?

All communities need rules, or laws, to guide the way people act toward each other. For example, there must be laws to keep a person from hurting someone else or taking another person's property. Laws for safe driving are needed to help prevent accidents on the highways. A community needs many different kinds of laws to help make it a safe and pleasant place in which to live.

Governments are needed to make laws. In every community, there must be a person or a group of persons to make the laws. Someone must also see that the laws are carried out. In other words, all communities need some form of government.

Governments do many things that make life better for people. They hire police officers to protect citizens from robbers and from other people who do not obey the laws. They also hire other workers, such as fire fighters and street cleaners. Governments build streets and sidewalks and keep them in repair. They provide parks and playgrounds where people can spend their free time. Some governments provide water for people to use in their homes. Also, governments have the job of running the schools in our communities.

To pay for all these services, large sums of money are needed. This money is raised through taxes which all citizens pay.

Just as every community needs some kind of government, so does every nation. In the United States, the national government has many important jobs to do. For example, it has the job of

defending our country from attack by enemies. It works together with other countries to solve important world problems. The national government prints the money we use for buying goods and services. It controls trade between people in the different states of our country. It makes rules to prevent pollution of our food, water, and air. It also helps people who cannot find jobs, or who for some other reason are not able to meet their basic needs.

- Each of the fifty states in our country has a government of its own. What jobs are done by the state governments? Look in other books to find the information you need.

A school board meeting. In most communities in the United States there is a group of people who have the job of running the public schools. Is the school board a part of the government? Explain. What other kinds of jobs are done by the government in your community?

Signing the Constitution. About fifty American leaders met in Philadelphia in the summer of 1787 to draw up a new plan of government for the United States. This plan is called the Constitution. Do you recognize any of the people in the picture above? If so, which ones?

■ How did the United States government begin?

About two hundred years ago, thirteen American colonies won their freedom from Great Britain during the Revolutionary War.*The colonies founded a new nation. They called it the United States of America.

The government of the new nation was very weak. It could pass laws for the United States, but it had no way to make sure that the laws were carried out. Each of the thirteen states was like a separate country. Each had its own government.

The Constitution was written. In May of 1787, a group of American leaders met in the city of Philadelphia. They wanted to see what could be done to make the government stronger. The leader of this meeting was George Washington. Among the other famous people who attended

*See Glossary

the meeting were Benjamin Franklin, James Madison, and Alexander Hamilton.

The people at the meeting decided to write a new plan of government for the United States. For almost four months, they argued about the kind of government that should be set up. There were many different ideas. Sometimes it seemed that the meeting would break up without reaching its goal. But at last the new plan, or Constitution, was ready. On September 17, 1787, thirty-nine people at the meeting signed the Constitution.

The Constitution became our plan of government. Before the new plan could go into effect, it had to be approved by at least nine of the thirteen states. Many people did not like the Constitution, because they thought it gave too much power to the national government. Other people were for the Constitution. They felt that a strong national government would be able to solve some of the country's problems.

By the summer of 1788, nine states had approved the Constitution. Now the new government was ready to begin work.

The Constitution proved to be very successful. Today—nearly two hundred years later—we still use the Constitution as our country's plan of government. In the meantime, the United States has become one of the largest and richest countries in the world.

- What do you think might have happened to the United States if the Constitution had not been approved?
- Do you think that the makers of the Constitution had to work together closely in order to reach their goal? Explain your answer.

■ What kind of government do we have in the United States today?

The United States has a federal system of government. This means that power is divided between the national government and the governments of the fifty states. The national government can do certain things that the state governments are not allowed to do. It can print money, and it can have an army and a navy. At the same time, the state governments can do certain things that the national government is not allowed to do.

Our national government is divided into three branches. One branch is called Congress. This is a group of men and women who make our country's laws. The second branch —headed by the president of the United States—carries out the laws made by Congress. The third branch is made up of federal courts. These

This picture shows a person learning to use a voting machine. In the United States, nearly all citizens can take part in elections for government leaders. What is a country with this kind of government called? Is it important for each citizen to vote in all elections? Why? Why not?

courts deal with cases that arise when our nation's laws are broken.

The American people have a large share in their government. Elections are held regularly to choose a president, a vice-president, and members of Congress. There are also elections to choose government leaders for states and smaller communities. In these elections, nearly all grown-ups can vote for the people they want to run the government. The people who receive the most votes are elected. A country with this kind of government is called a democracy.

- Is it important for the citizens of a democracy to know what is going on in their government? Explain.
- Would it be possible to have a democracy if the people did not have a large amount of freedom? Why? Why not?
- You belong to several different groups, such as your family and your school class. Which of these groups decide things by voting?

The right-hand picture below shows Ella Grasso and her husband at a victory party. Mrs. Grasso became governor of Connecticut in 1974 because she received more votes than any other person. Do you think this is a fair way of choosing government leaders? Explain.

An **American astronaut** (Edwin Aldrin, Jr.) carrying out an experiment on the surface of the moon. Why is he wearing a space suit? What is the large object behind him? Although the sun is shining, the sky overhead is as black as night. What do you think is the reason for this?

3 Cooperation

■ How did cooperation help to put people on the moon?

July 20, 1969, was an exciting day for millions of people all over the world. On that day, two American astronauts—Neil Armstrong and Edwin Aldrin, Jr.—became the first persons to land on the moon.

These two men could never have made the journey to the moon all by themselves. They needed the help of many other people.

First, there had to be scientists who could figure out a way of getting people to the moon. These people had to solve many hard problems. For example, a spacecraft must move very rapidly to overcome the powerful force that pulls everything toward the earth. This force is known as gravity. The spacecraft must be able to slow down and land safely on the moon. It must also be able to take off to make the journey back to earth.

It is very cold in space. There is no air for people to breathe. Also, the sun gives off certain rays that can be harmful. People had to plan space suits and other equipment needed to protect the astronauts.

Large amounts of money were needed to pay for the spacecraft and the other things used by the astronauts. The United States government provided this money. Most of the money came from taxes paid by citizens all over our country.

The government did not make the equipment for the moon journey. Instead, a number of companies were hired by the government to do the work. Some companies built different parts of the spacecraft. Others made the space suits. Still other companies made radios, cameras, and other things to go inside the spacecraft. Thousands of people were put to work making all of these different things.

The people who were in charge of the space flight had to be sure that nothing would go wrong. If an accident took place, the astronauts might be killed. For this reason, everything that the astronauts used

Factory workers putting electrical wires into a spacecraft. Why do you suppose so many wires are needed? Do you think these people must work together to do a good job? Explain. What might happen if one of the persons who worked on a spacecraft failed to do his or her part?

had to be tested very carefully. Before the moon journey, a number of astronauts took shorter trips into space to make sure that all of the equipment worked properly.

The first moon visit was very successful. The American astronauts spent about two hours walking around the lifeless surface of the moon. They carried out experi-

ments and gathered soil and rocks to take back for tests. They also put up an American flag. When their spacecraft took off for the journey back to earth, the astronauts left behind a metal sign that said, "We came in peace for all mankind."

Since that time, several other astronauts have landed on the moon. They have brought back much new information about our nearest neighbor in space. Someday, astronauts may be able to visit Mars and other planets.*

- Working together is called cooperation. Do you think the first moon flight could have been made if people had not been willing to cooperate? Give reasons for your answer.

- Did the American astronauts need to work together in order to make a safe journey to the moon? What might have happened if they had not cooperated with each other?

*See Glossary

A spacecraft ready to be used on a journey to the moon. How do you think these workers will feel if the space flight is successful? Will they feel that they did their work well? Explain. What are some other important goals that people can reach by working together?

■ In what ways did the American Indians work together?

As you know, all people on earth have certain needs they must meet in order to be healthy and happy. The three kinds of basic needs are described on pages 130-131.

No person can meet his or her needs all alone. Every person must have the help of other people. Of course, you should not expect to get this help unless you are willing to help other people in return. Only by working together can people meet their basic needs.

Cooperation in hunting communities. Cooperation was used by the Indians who made their homes in

A **Plains Indian camp.** Many different tribes of Indians lived on the wide plains in the central part of North America. How did these Indians cooperate with one another to meet their needs?

North America long ago. Among these people were the Plains Indians. They lived on the wide plains that stretch from the Mississippi River to the Rocky Mountains. Great herds of buffalo roamed this grassy land. The Plains Indians depended on the buffalo to provide many things they needed. Buffalo meat was their main food. They used buffalo skins for covering their tents, or tepees. Buffalo skins were also used to make robes, shoes, and other articles of clothing.

The Plains Indians worked together to hunt buffalo. Sometimes a group of hunters would form a big circle around a buffalo herd. Then they would kill the buffalo with spears or with bows and arrows. Afterwards, the women of the community would work together to cut up the dead buffalo for meat.

Cooperation in farming communities. People in farming communities also had to cooperate with each other. For example, the Hopi Indians lived on a high plain in what is now the state of Arizona. The Hopi grew corn, beans, and other crops for food. All of the people in a community worked together to plant and harvest their crops.

- Are there any important jobs in a community that can be done without cooperation? If so, what are they?
- Would it be possible for any community to get along without cooperation? Give facts to back up your answer.

Building a house. This picture was taken in the old town of Williamsburg, Virginia. Part of Williamsburg has been rebuilt to look much as it did in colonial days. The American colonists often helped each other to build houses and barns. Why do you suppose they did this?

■ How did the American colonists use cooperation?

About four hundred years ago, people from England and other European countries began coming to America to live. As time passed, thirteen English colonies grew up along the Atlantic coast.

The American colonists had to work very hard to meet their needs for food, clothing, and shelter. They found that many hard jobs were easier and more enjoyable when peo-

ple worked together. For example, a group of women would sometimes come to a neighbor's house to sew a patchwork* quilt. While the women worked, they enjoyed talking and laughing together. This kind of get-together was called a "quilting bee." Another type of party was the "husking bee," like the one shown in the picture on page 35. There were also plowing bees and house-cleaning bees. When a new family moved into a community, the neighbors would get together to help them build a house.

The people in the American colonies were always ready to help one another in case of trouble. For instance, a farmer might be sick or injured. Then his neighbors would do his farm chores until he was able to work again.

- Do you think that people from Europe could have built communities in America if they had not been willing to cooperate with each other? Explain your answer.
- Why is life usually more pleasant and satisfying when people work together?

A husking bee was a type of party held in colonial times. Neighbors would get together to remove the husks from the corn they had grown. Do you think it would be fun to take part in a husking bee? What are some other ways in which the colonists helped each other?

■ Why is cooperation needed in our government?

Today, people in America still need to work together in order to reach their goals. For example, there must be cooperation among the people who are in charge of our country's government.

Making the laws. The laws of our nation are made by the United States Congress. This group of people is made up of two smaller groups, the Senate and the House of Representatives. Before a law can be put into use, it must be approved by more than half of the people in both the Senate and the House of Representatives. If the members of Congress were not willing to work together, it would not be possible to make the laws that our country needs.

Carrying out the laws. The president of the United States is in charge of carrying out the laws that Congress has made. To do this, the president needs thousands of helpers. These workers are grouped into a number of different departments, such as the Department of Defense and the Department of the Treasury. The people of all these departments must cooperate with one another in order to do a good job of carrying out the laws.

State laws. As you know, our country is divided into fifty states. Each state has a group of lawmakers like the United States Congress. Each state also has a governor, who is in charge of carrying out the state laws.

- Do you think that the people who are in charge of the state governments must cooperate with each other in order to do their jobs well? Explain.
- Can you think of some problems in government that might come about if people do not cooperate? Tell about these problems.

The **Michigan House of Representatives** helps to make laws for the state of Michigan. Another group of lawmakers in Michigan is called the Senate. In many ways, these groups are like the United States Senate and House of Representatives. Who makes the laws in the state where you live? Look in your school library for information that will help you answer this question.

■ How does cooperation help communities and families?

Communities. In communities all over our nation, people work together to reach important goals. Here are some examples:

. . . A group of citizens might join together to ask the city government to build a new playground in their neighborhood.

. . . The members of a church might work together to repair their church building and give it a new coat of paint.

. . . Some parents of school students might cooperate to raise money for new band uniforms.

Many jobs take so much time and work that they cannot be done by one person working alone. They can only be done by a group of people working together. When people co-

Cleaning trash out of a stream. These young people are working together to make their community a better place in which to live. Do you think this job is worthwhile? Why? Why not? What important jobs in your own community have been done through cooperation?

operate on jobs like these, they get a feeling of satisfaction from working with others who share their ideas and goals.

Families. Cooperation is also important to families. Usually the parents of a family work together. They see that their children have food, clothing, and shelter. The children often help their parents around the house. They do jobs such as washing the dishes or mowing the lawn. Older brothers and sisters may help younger children with their homework. They may also teach them new skills, such as playing baseball or using a hammer. By working together, the members of a family can have a more enjoyable life.

- Can you think of some goals that you can reach only by cooperating with others? If so, what are they?
- What do people have to do in order to work together successfully? Do they need to be friendly and polite? Must they be able to work hard without complaining? Give facts to back up your answers.
- In what ways do you cooperate with other people in your family?

A family taking a canoe ride. Is a family a kind of community? Explain. Why is life more pleasant and satisfying when family members work together?

George Washington and his soldiers at Valley Forge. Where is Valley Forge, and what happened there? What does this picture tell you about the American soldiers who were at Valley Forge?

4 Loyalty

■ How did loyalty help the United States to win its independence?

A freezing wind blew over the tiny village of Valley Forge, Pennsylvania. It whistled through cracks in people's houses and piled the snow into deep drifts. Outside the town, some tired-looking soldiers in ragged clothing stood around a smoky campfire. They stamped their feet and beat their hands together in order to keep warm.

It was December, 1777, and the American colonists were fighting a war to gain their freedom from Great Britain. A short time before this, British soldiers had captured the important city of Philadelphia. George Washington, the leader of the American army, decided that his soldiers should set up camp at Valley Forge. This town was only about twenty-five miles from Philadelphia, but it was not likely that the British would attack the Americans during the cold winter months.

The soldiers who were at Valley Forge that winter faced many hardships. At that time, the American government did not have much money. It could not buy all the supplies the army needed. The soldiers often did not have enough food. Some also went without shoes or coats. The soldiers had to live in rough log cabins that they built themselves. Many of them died from smallpox or other serious diseases.

It is not surprising that some of the soldiers gave up and went home. Many more would have left if it had not been for General Washington. Day after day, he rode through the camp. His strength and courage helped to keep the little army together.

All winter long, the soldiers practiced military drills. By spring, the army was well trained and ready to fight the British again. The Revolutionary War lasted for several more years. Finally, the British leaders decided that the Americans could not be defeated. They agreed to treat the United States as an independent nation.

- Do you think that the soldiers at Valley Forge were loyal to their country? Give reasons for your answer.
- How did General Washington show loyalty to his soldiers? Why is it important for leaders to be loyal to the people who follow them?
- Could the United States have become an independent country if Americans had not been loyal to certain ideas and beliefs? Explain your answer.

■ What part did loyalty play in the life of Jane Addams?

During the early 1900's, one of the most famous people in America was Jane Addams of Chicago, Illinois. This great woman spent most of her life helping poor people who lived in city slums.*

Jane Addams was born in 1860 in the small town of Cedarville, Illinois. Her father was a well-to-do businessman. When Jane was about six years old, her father took her on a business trip to a mill. Near the

*See Glossary

Jane Addams spent most of her life helping poor people in Chicago. This picture shows her telling a story to a group of children at Hull House, the place where she lived and worked.

factory, Jane saw poor people and run-down houses for the first time in her life. The sight made her very sad. "When I grow up," Jane told her father, "I am going to build a great, big house and live right by horrid houses like these. Then I will let the people come in to see me for help."

Jane also planned to be a doctor when she grew up. After graduating from Rockford College in 1881, she entered medical school. But the next year she became ill and had to leave. To get back her health, she visited Europe. In London, she stayed in a house much like the one she had wanted when she was a girl. She decided to carry out her childhood plan after her return to the United States.

In 1889, Jane moved into a large brick house in a poor, shabby neighborhood of Chicago. It was called Hull House, after the man who had built it. Jane invited people in the

Today Jane Addams' work is carried on by the Hull House Association. This group offers classes and other programs for people of all ages. A music class is shown in the picture below.

neighborhood to come to Hull House any time they wanted. There they could take classes in cooking, sewing, woodworking, and other useful skills. People who moved here from other countries could learn to speak and write English. Children could come to Hull House to play games and listen to stories. There was a kindergarten and nursery school for the younger children. People who needed food or medical care could get help at Hull House.

As time passed, many people gave free time or money to help Jane Addams with her work. So many people came to Hull House that new buildings were needed. Soon, Hull House covered a whole city block.

Besides her work at Hull House, Jane Addams helped people in many other ways. For example, she helped improve working conditions in factories and to clean up dirty streets and alleys in Chicago. Through her work, the first court for children only was started in Chicago. People from many countries listened to her speak on the problems of the poor. Many people also read the books and magazine articles she wrote about these problems.

During her lifetime, Jane Addams worked hard to bring about peace

Pledge to the Flag

I pledge allegiance to the flag of the United States of America and to the Republic for which it stands, one Nation under God, indivisible, with liberty and justice for all.

among all countries. In 1915 she helped form a group for world peace. Partly because of this work, she received the Nobel Peace Prize* in 1931. President Theodore Roosevelt once called her "America's most useful citizen."

- Do you think Jane Addams was loyal to certain beliefs and ideas? If so, what were they? How did Jane Addams show her loyalty?
- Was Jane Addams loyal to the people who came to Hull House? Explain your answer.

Schoolchildren saluting the American flag. To the left of the picture is the Pledge to the Flag, which many children say in school every day. Do you think saluting the flag and saying the Pledge are good ways for people to show their loyalty to the United States? Explain.

■ How do Americans show loyalty to their country?

In the United States today, most people have a strong feeling of loyalty toward their country. They are also loyal to certain ideas and beliefs on which the nation was founded. For example, most Americans are loyal to the ideas of democracy and freedom. In addition, most Americans are loyal to their government leaders, and their leaders are usually loyal to them.

There are many ways in which Americans show their loyalty to the United States. They honor the American flag by flying it on national holidays and saluting it when it goes by in a parade. They say the Pledge to the Flag and they stand at attention when our national anthem, "The Star-Spangled Banner," is played.

Americans also show loyalty to their country by being good citizens.

They are careful to obey the laws of the nation and of the community in which they live. They give money and hours of hard work to carry out projects that will help everyone in the community. If they are asked to serve on a jury,* they do it willingly. They pay their fair share of taxes. Good citizens vote in all elections. (See page 27.) They try to find out about important matters, so they can vote wisely and help to elect good leaders.

Most Americans show their loyalty to the ideas of freedom and justice for all people. They try to treat every person alike. They want other Americans to have the same rights and freedoms that they themselves enjoy.

Many Americans show their loyalty to the United States by serving in our country's armed forces. In times of war, thousands of loyal citizens have even given their lives in order to keep our nation strong and free.

- How would you explain the Pledge to the Flag in your own words? A dictionary and other books will help you answer this question.
- Why is it important for people to be loyal to their country?

- Could any nation last for very long if it did not have loyal citizens? Explain your answer.
- Do you think that <u>you</u> are a loyal citizen of your country? Why? Why not? What are some of the ways in which you show your loyalty?
- What if your nation's government did something that you believe is wrong? Should you still be loyal to the nation? Give reasons for your answer.

■ What other kinds of loyalty do Americans have?

Long ago, people discovered that they had to be loyal to one another in order to live together successfully in communities. In every community, there were a number of hard or unpleasant tasks that had to be done for the good of everyone. People would never have been willing to do these tasks unless they felt a strong sense of loyalty to the community. Members of families had to be loyal to each other in order to have a happy family life.

In the United States today, most people are loyal in a number of different ways. They are loyal to the members of their family and to their friends. They are also loyal to the

A Roman Catholic worship service in Chicago. Do you think these people are being loyal to their religious faith? Explain your answer. Are there certain beliefs or ideas to which you are loyal? If so, what are they? How do you show your loyalty to these beliefs or ideas?

clubs and groups to which they belong. For example, a student may be loyal to the school band, the football team, or a scout troop. A grownup may be loyal to a group such as the Lions Club or the League of Women Voters.

Most Americans are also loyal to their work. They show their loyalty by trying to do their job as well as possible, without complaining. They know that their job makes it possible for them to earn money with which to buy the things they need and want.

Many people in our country are loyal to their religious faith. They show their loyalty by attending services at a church, a temple, or some other place of worship. They give time and money to help carry out important church projects. They try to follow the rules of their religion and to treat other people the way they themselves would like to be treated.

Eating breakfast. Do you think the members of this family are loyal to each other? What makes you think this? Is loyalty important to families everywhere? Explain your answer.

Do you think that the teacher in this picture is loyal to her students? Are her students loyal to her? Could there be a good school without loyal teachers and students? Give reasons for your answers.

- Do all persons need friends that they can trust? Give reasons for your answer. What are some ways in which you can show loyalty to your friends?
- How do you show your loyalty to your parents? To other members of your family? How do they show their loyalty to you?
- Can you disagree with a friend or a member of your family and still be loyal to that person? Explain your answer.
- Do you think that loyalty is needed in sports? Why? Why not? How can a player show loyalty to his or her team?
- Why is it important for people to be loyal to their jobs? What do you think would happen if workers were not loyal?
- Can people show loyalty by the things they say as well as by the things they do? Explain.

The last half of the ninth inning, with the bases loaded. What do you suppose the catcher is saying to the pitcher? If you could not speak any language, how would you let people know your ideas and feelings?

5 Language

■ How does language help people to meet their needs?

In order to live and work together, people must be able to communicate—that is, to let others know their ideas and feelings. They can do this in a number of different ways. For example, they can make motions with their hands. Or they can draw pictures. But most of the time, people use words to communicate with each other. Sometimes these words are spoken. Sometimes they are written or printed. Together, all the words used by a group of people make up a language. Language might be called a golden key that helps people to live together in communities.

Language is also important for another reason. If you have ever tried to solve a hard problem, you may have discovered that you were "talking to yourself." Even if you were not saying words out loud, you were forming words in your mind. This made it easier for you to think about your problem. Some scientists believe that without language, people would not be able to think at all.

In a school library. How are these students using language? What do you think it would be like to live in a community where only a few people knew how to read and write? If people cannot read and write, is it harder for them to meet their needs? Explain.

Although people everywhere use words to communicate with each other, they do not all use the same language. More than three thousand different languages are spoken on the earth today. Some of these languages are used by only a small number of persons. Other languages—such as English, Spanish, and Chinese—are used by millions of people.

- What language do you speak at home? How did you learn this language? How does your language help you to meet your needs?

- Think about your parents and other grown-ups you know. What kinds of work do they do? Would they be able to do their jobs successfully without using language? Explain your answer.

- How do people who speak different languages communicate?

A **Sioux Indian** painting on a buffalo skin. Each picture stands for an important event in the history of the tribe. Do you think this was a good way of communicating?

■ How did the American Indians communicate?

Like all other people on earth, the American Indians had to communicate with each other in order to meet their needs. They did this mainly by talking to one another.

More than two hundred different languages were spoken by the Indians in what is now the United States and Canada. Some of these languages were much like each other, but some were as different as English and Chinese are. To communicate with people who spoke a different language, some tribes made motions with their hands. For example, two hands clasped together stood for "peace."

The Indians who lived in this part of North America did not have any written language. As a result, it was hard to store information for use at a later time. Some tribes used a form of picture writing. They drew pictures on birchbark or animal skins to show important events in their history. Some tribes used belts made out of seashells to keep a record of agreements they had made with other tribes.

Without a written language, it was also hard for the Indians to communicate over long distances. Sometimes they used smoke signals or drum beats to send a message from one place to another. However, only very short messages could be sent in this way.

- Why do you suppose the Indians of North America spoke so many different languages?
- If you lived in a community where there was no written language, how could you keep track of things you wanted to remember at a later time? How could you send a message to a person who lived far away?

What ways of communicating were used in earlier times?

During the 1600's and 1700's, large numbers of settlers came to America from Europe. Like the Indians, these people often communicated by talking to each other. But they also had a way of writing.

The first written languages appeared in Egypt and in southwestern Asia about five thousand years ago. Writing made it possible for people to store information to be used later. By writing, people could send messages to others who were far away.

For thousands of years, all writing was done by hand. It took months to make a single copy of a book. Because of this, books cost so much that only a few people could buy them. Printing was first invented* in China about twelve hundred years ago. But news of this invention did not reach Europe.

An important invention. In the 1400's, a man in Germany named Johann Gutenberg* invented a printing press that used metal* type. With this machine, many copies of a book could be made in a short time. Books became cheap enough so that many people could buy them.

The first printing press in the American colonies was set up in Massachusetts about 1639. As time passed, many printing shops were set up in the colonies. They printed mainly religious books and school books. Some of them also printed newspapers. The first successful newspaper in America was the *Boston News-Letter*. It was started in 1704. By the time of the Revolutionary War (1775), there were a number of newspapers in the thirteen colonies. They printed news about things that happened all over the world.

Communication in colonial times. In colonial days, it took a long time to send a message from one place to another. Letters were usually carried on horseback or on ships at sea. Sometimes it took three or four months for a message to get from England to the American colonies. Even sending a letter from one colony to another might take a month.

In colonial cities and towns, news was spread in several ways. Most often, friends and neighbors told each other the news. In some towns, important notices were posted in public places. Many communities had a person called a town crier. He would walk through the streets ringing a bell. When a crowd had gathered, the town crier would tell them the news.

*See Glossary

A colonial printing shop. This picture was taken in the old part of Williamsburg, Virginia, which has been rebuilt to look as it did about 250 years ago. The large machine on the right is a printing press. Why were printing presses important to the American colonies?

- Why did people own few books before the time of Gutenberg?
- Do you think the invention of printing made it easier for people in Europe to meet their needs? Explain your answer.
- How were ways of communicating in colonial times different from those we use today?

A pony express rider changing to a fresh horse at a relay station in the West. What was the pony express, and how did it work? Why was it in business for only a year and a half? Look in other books to find more information that will help you answer these questions.

■ What changes have taken place in communication?

The United States became a nation about two hundred years ago. Since that time, important changes have taken place in the ways people communicate with each other. Let us see how these changes came about.

The telegraph. Until the 1840's, a person who wanted to communicate with someone far away had to go there in person or write a letter. Then an American artist named Samuel Morse invented a way of sending messages by wires. This was the telegraph. Before long, telegraph lines connected all the main cities in the United States. In 1866, a telegraph cable* was laid under the Atlantic Ocean. Now it was possible to send messages instantly between Europe and North America.

The telephone. The next important new way of communicating was

the telephone. It was invented in the 1870's by Alexander Graham Bell. People could use the telephone to talk with friends and relatives who lived far away. They could call doctors, police officers, or fire fighters when they needed help. Business people could talk with customers who were far away. By 1900, more than one million telephones were being used in the United States.

Transportation. About the same time, new means of transportation were making it possible to carry letters

"Mr. Watson, come here. I want you!" This was the first message ever sent by telephone. One day in 1876, Alexander Graham Bell was carrying out some experiments with his new invention, the telephone. When he spilled a chemical on his clothing, he called to his assistant, Thomas Watson. Even though Watson was in another room, he could hear Bell's voice clearly over the telephone. How did this invention change the American people's way of living?

much faster than before. For example, railroads were built in most parts of the United States during the 1800's. The first automobiles were made in the 1890's, and the first airplanes a few years later. Today, mail is carried from place to place in trucks, trains, and airplanes. An airmail letter can be sent all the way across the country in a few hours.

The phonograph and motion pictures. During the late 1800's, the famous inventor Thomas Edison helped to develop two important means of communication. These are the phonograph and motion pictures. The phonograph makes it possible to record human voices and other sounds. Then they can be heard at a later time. With motion picture cameras, people take moving pictures of events as they are actually happening.

Radio. In 1895 an Italian inventor named Guglielmo Marconi* found a way to send messages through the air without using wires. He called this the wireless telegraph. The "wireless" was especially useful for communicating with ships at sea.

In the early 1900's, the wireless telegraph led to the radio. Through radio, it was possible to send the

human voice over long distances without using wires as a telephone does. In 1920, the first radio station in the world began broadcasting in the city of Pittsburgh, Pennsylvania. Soon people in the United States were listening to the news and other programs on their own radio sets.

Television. Another important invention was television. The first regular television programs were broadcast in the 1940's. With television, people can stay home and watch events that are happening in other places.

During recent years, science has brought even more changes in communication. For example, messages can now be sent to far-off places with the help of space satellites.*

- Why do you suppose so many new ways of communicating have been developed since the invention of the telegraph?
- How have the new ways of communicating helped us to learn more about the world around us? How have they changed the communities in which we live?

Producing a television show. Television is one of several new ways of communicating. What are some of the others?

6 Education

■ Why is education important to every person?

Have you ever watched a spider spinning a web? This is a job that appears to take much skill. Perhaps you wondered how the spider ever learned to spin its web. The answer is that a spider does not have to <u>learn</u> this job. It is born with the ability to spin webs.

A way of behaving that does not have to be learned is sometimes called an instinct. Nearly all animals depend on instincts to meet their needs for food and shelter. Instincts also help protect them from their enemies.

Why must human* beings learn? Human beings are different from other animals in many ways. For one thing, they have very few instincts to tell them what to do. Instead, they must learn the things they have to know to meet their needs. They can do this because they have larger and better brains. Unlike other animals, human beings can think and decide things for themselves.

Learning is important to human beings for several reasons. First, it helps them meet their physical needs, such as the need for food and clothing. (See pages 130-131.) In our country today, most people use

*See Glossary

money to buy food and other things they need. To earn money, they work at many different kinds of jobs. For most of these jobs, there are skills that must be learned.

Learning also helps people to meet their social needs. (See pages 130-131.) All human beings need to belong to a group of people who like and respect each other. But in order

to get along with other people, they must follow certain rules. These rules have to be learned. Also, every person has certain talents and abilities. People must develop and use their abilities to be happy and successful in life. They cannot do this without learning.

There is still another reason why learning is important to human beings. Scientists say that most people —even as babies—want to know about the world around them. Learning helps them to satisfy this natural curiosity.

Learning from others. People can learn many things by themselves. But they must also learn from others. Ever since human beings have lived in communities, the older people have passed on their knowledge and skills to the younger people.

Children learning how a plant grows. Do you think most people are born with a deep desire to learn about the world in which they live? Give facts to back up your answer.

This is one reason why human beings have been able to make so much progress. They can use the knowledge and skills of the people who lived before they did.

Helping people learn is known as education. This is one of the great ideas that have helped to build our nation.

- Do you think it would be possible for any person to meet her or his needs without education? Explain.

- Do you think that communities need educated people? Explain.

Chippewa Indians building a house called a wigwam out of poles and birchbark. Do you think these people knew how to build wigwams from the time they were babies, or did they have to learn this skill? If they had to learn this skill, who do you suppose taught them?

■ How did young people learn in Indian days?

Like all other people, the Indians long ago had to learn many things. But there were no schools or teachers then. Instead, parents taught their children most of the things they had to know. For example, an Indian father might teach his son how to hunt and fish. He might also teach his son how to defend himself against his enemies. An Indian mother might teach her daughter how to grow corn and other crops. She might also teach her how to cook and sew.

Indian children also learned many things from other grown-ups. For instance, one of the old men in the tribe might teach the young men how to take part in certain ceremonies. These were supposed to bring good luck in hunting.

Sometimes children learned certain skills from their older brothers and sisters. For example, their brothers and sisters might teach them how to play games. They might also teach them how to get along with other people. Children might also learn useful skills from other young people in the community.

The Indian tribes of North America did not use any form of writing. But of course all of them had a spoken language. Just like young people today, Indian children learned to talk by listening to their parents and other people.

- Was education as important to the Indians long ago as it is to people today? Give reasons for your answer.
- How was education in Indian days like the education that you know about today? How was it different?

■ What were schools like in the early days of our country?

When the first English colonies were started in America, there were no school buildings and no teachers. Families often lived miles apart and roads were poor. Because of this, it would have been very hard for most children to get to a school. Also, children had to help with the farm work and the household chores. They had little time to learn reading and writing. Most children learned what they needed to know from their parents.

The first schools. In spite of these problems, many people in the colonies wanted to start schools. This was especially true of the Pilgrims* and other religious groups in New England.* They believed that everyone should be able to read the Bible. They thought this would help people become better Christians.

The first schools in New England were called "dame schools." These schools were held in people's homes. A woman would gather the neighborhood children around her fireplace. Then she would teach them how to read, write, and spell. While the children were studying their lessons, she would do her spinning or weaving.

In 1647, an important law was passed in Massachusetts. It said that every town of fifty or more families had to set up a school to teach reading and writing. Towns with one hundred or more families had to have a "Latin* school." This school would prepare students for college. Later, other colonies in New England passed laws like this one.

In colonial days, girls were not thought to be as smart as boys. They could learn reading and writing, but

A country school in the 1800's. In what ways is this school like the one that you attend? In what ways is it different? What subjects do you suppose these children are studying?

they were not allowed to go to Latin school.

Settlers in the Middle Colonies* also started schools. However, there were almost no schools at all in the Southern Colonies.* It was hard to start schools there. Families lived far away from each other. Also, many people in the Southern Colonies did not believe that all children needed an education. Sometimes wealthy planters hired teachers from England to teach their children. But boys and girls from poor families had few chances to go to school.

In colonial days, most schools were dark and unpleasant. Usually they were very small and had only one teacher. Children of all ages studied together in one room. They sat on hard wooden benches. Teachers were very strict. They would often whip the children if they were noisy or made mistakes. Students usually had to attend school six days a week. Classes began at seven or eight o'clock in the morning. They did not end until four or five o'clock in the afternoon.

The first American college. In 1636, Massachusetts started the first college in the American colonies. This was Harvard College, which later became a university.* By the late 1700's, there were eighteen colleges and universities in the colonies. Most of these had been started by churches to train young men to become ministers. Only men went to college in colonial times. Wealthy people usually sent their sons to universities in England.

- Why were the Pilgrims and other religious groups in America so interested in starting schools?
- Do you think you would rather attend a colonial school or a school like the one you go to today? Explain.

■ How did education change during the 1800's?

In 1776 the United States became an independent country. Now the American people were free to run their own government. It was more important than ever for them to have a good education.

For many years, however, little was done to provide better schools. Even in New England, most schools were not free. Parents had to pay to send their children to school. As a result, many children never went to school at all. The school year was much shorter than it is today. Classes would be held for only a few weeks in summer. Then they would be held for a few more weeks in winter. Teachers were poorly paid, and had very little training.

A fight for better schools. Many Americans felt that better schools were needed. One of these was a lawyer in Massachusetts named Horace Mann. In 1837, he helped pass a law that set up a state board of education. For twelve years, he served as secretary of this board.

Mann knew that his hardest job was to make people want better schools. He traveled all over Massachusetts making speeches. In his speeches, he explained why it was so important to have good schools. He also said that these schools should be free to all children. Each year, Mann wrote a report about the schools in Massachusetts. In these reports, he made suggestions for better schools and better ways of teaching. Mann also helped to start a college where teachers could be trained for their jobs. The changes

Mann brought about in Massachusetts soon spread to other states.

Changes in education. During the 1800's, many other changes took place in education. For example, the first state universities in our country were started around 1800. These were in North Carolina and Georgia. Boston, Massachusetts, started the first public high school in our country in 1821. In 1852, Massachusetts passed a law saying that all children of a certain age must attend school. This was the first law of its kind in our country. Today, nearly all states have such laws.

- Why do you suppose so many changes in education took place in the 1800's? Was there a greater need for education than there had been in earlier times? Explain your answer.
- Nearly all states today have laws saying that all children must attend school. Why do you think such laws were passed?

Horace Mann speaking to lawmakers in Massachusetts. How did Horace Mann help to bring about changes in American education? Do you think these changes were good ones? Explain.

■ How do young people learn what they need to know today?

At the present time, most people in the United States have the chance to get a good education. There are many fine schools in all parts of our country. Most of these are public schools, which are free to all students. The money to run these schools comes from taxes that people pay to the government. In addition, there are many private schools in the United States. The private schools are not run with tax money as the public schools are. Instead, most of them are run with money that comes from churches or other groups. Also, the parents usually pay fees for sending their children to these schools.

Grade school students in a science class. Where do you suppose money comes from to build schools and hire teachers? What is the difference between public and private schools?

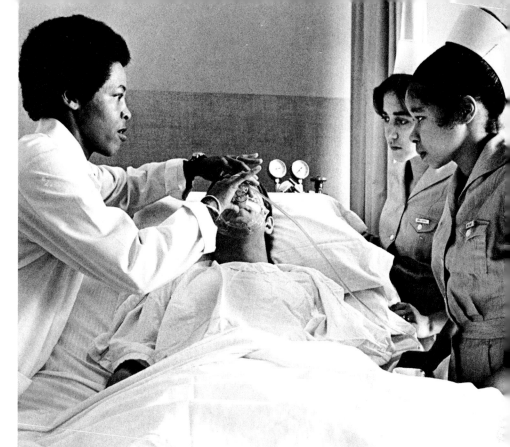

Student nurses with their instructor at a college in New York City. These students are learning how to care for sick people. Why do all communities need people who are well trained for their jobs?

Today, children in most parts of the United States must begin school by the age of seven. They must attend school until they are at least sixteen. After grade school, most young people go on to high school. Also, many children attend nursery school before starting grade school.

Millions of Americans today continue their education after high school. Many go to colleges or universities. Others go to schools where they can learn the skills they need for certain jobs. For example, there are business schools, art schools, and schools of nursing.

Many people who work at full-time jobs are now getting more education. They want to learn new skills or to have a more satisfying life. Some attend classes during their spare time.

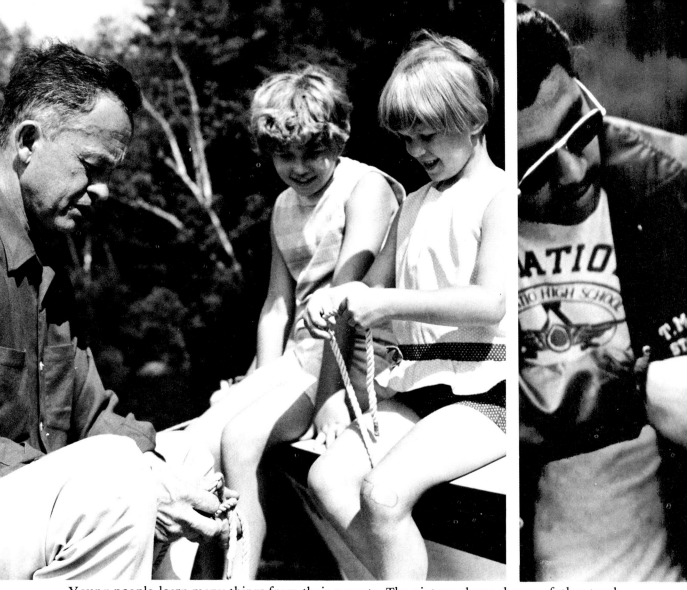

Young people learn many things from their parents. The picture above shows a father teaching his daughters how to tie knots. How do you think this skill might be useful to them?

Not all education today takes place in schools. Just as in earlier times, young people learn many things from their families. For example, you probably learned to talk by listening to your parents or to older brothers and sisters. Perhaps the members of your family have also taught you a number of different skills. These might include telling time, riding a bicycle, baking a cake, and playing football.

Young people also learn many things from other people in the community. Most churches have Sunday schools or special classes where children can learn about their religion. Scouts, 4-H clubs, and other groups also help to educate young people. Coaches, youth workers, and other

In the picture above, a high school coach is showing one of his students how to use a bow and arrow. Do you think this man enjoys what he is doing? Give reasons for your answer.

grown-ups help boys and girls learn useful skills.

People today have other ways of learning things they need to know. They can find out many things by reading books, magazines, and newspapers. Public libraries have much useful information. Today, radio and television help millions of people enjoy learning.

- What are some of the things you have learned in school? From your family? From books and newspapers? From radio and television? Do you think that the things you have learned outside school are an important part of your education? Why? Why not?

- Do you think it is important for democratic* countries like the United States to have citizens who are well educated? Explain.

Making maple syrup and sugar. What natural resources do you think the Indians in this picture are using? Are these same resources still used by people in the United States today? Explain.

7 Using Natural Resources

■ How did the American Indians use natural resources?

Ever since people first lived on the earth, they have used many things they have found in the world around them to meet their needs. These "gifts of nature" are called natural resources. Among the most important kinds of natural resources are:

• Sunshine
• Air
• Water
• Soil
• Minerals *
• Wild plants (including trees)
• Wild animals (including fish)

*See Glossary

The Indians who lived in North America long ago used all these different kinds of resources. Most tribes hunted wild animals such as deer, buffalo, ducks, and rabbits for food. They also caught fish. Often the Indians used the skins and furs of the animals they killed to make their clothing. Animal bones were used to make knives, needles, and other tools. Some Indian tribes on the plains used buffalo skins to cover their tepees.

The Indians also found many ways of using trees and other wild plants. They gathered fruit, berries, nuts, seeds, and roots to use for food. Some tribes collected the sap from maple trees and boiled it until it became thick maple syrup or chunks of brown sugar. To build a house, many Indian tribes first made a framework of poles. Then they covered the poles with bark, leaves, or grass. Other tribes built houses from logs or wooden planks. Wood was also used to make different tools and weapons, such as hoes, axes, bows, and arrows. Nearly all of the Indians built fires from wood to cook their meals and heat their houses. Some tribes used birchbark to make canoes. Others made boats from hollow logs.

As you discovered earlier, some Indians in North America raised crops. These crops needed sunshine, water, and good soil.

The Indians of North America also used minerals to meet their needs. For instance, clay was used in making dishes and pots. Some tribes made bricks from clay that had been dried in the sun. They used these bricks to build their houses. Other tribes built houses from stone or from hard-packed earth. The

Indians put salt on their food to make it taste better. They used hard stones in making arrows and tomahawks.* Some tribes dug copper from the earth and used it to make knives or jewelry.

- Do you think the Indians could have met their needs for food, clothing, and shelter without using natural resources? Give facts to back up your answer.
- Do you think the Indians used natural resources in as many different ways as people do today? Explain.

■ What part did iron and other metals play in our nation's history?

When settlers from Europe began coming to America, they brought new ways of using natural resources. For example, these people knew how to get iron, copper, and other useful metals from certain kinds of ore.* One way of doing this was to heat the ore over a fire made from charcoal. The charcoal burned with a very hot flame,

Making pots from iron in colonial days. Iron was heated until it melted. Then it was molded into different shapes to make tools and other articles. What natural resources did the colonists use in making iron?

Steel workers in Pennsylvania in 1895. About 1860, factories in the United States began to use new ways of making steel. How did this change the American people's way of living? In the following pages, you will discover facts that can help answer this question.

causing the ore to melt. Then it was quite easy to separate the metal from the rest of the ore.

Making iron. The settlers found that their new homeland was rich in the natural resources needed to make iron. In some places, there were large deposits* of iron ore. Also, America had huge forests that could supply wood for making charcoal. Rivers provided water to cool the hot iron and wash away the other materials in the ore. The flowing water could also be used to turn large water wheels, which provided the power to run machinery.

Inside a modern steel plant. The thing that looks like a huge kettle in this picture is full of hot, melted steel. The workers are preparing to pour the steel into molds. In what ways is this factory like the one shown in the picture on pages 74-75? In what ways is it different?

As time passed, the settlers built a number of ironworks* in the American colonies. The iron produced here was used to make tools, guns, and other useful articles. By the time of the Revolutionary War, the colonists were making enough iron to meet most of their own needs.

Making steel. For hundreds of years, people had known about a special kind of iron called steel. They knew that steel is much stronger and more useful than ordinary iron. But in colonial times it was very difficult and costly to make. For this reason, only small amounts of steel were produced each year.

During the 1800's, people in Europe and the United States discovered some new ways of making steel. These new ways made it possible to produce huge amounts of steel quickly and cheaply. During the years that followed, many large steel mills were built in different parts of the United States.

An important industry. Today, the making of iron and steel is one of our country's most important industries. Millions of people work in steel plants or in factories that use iron and steel to make other useful products. Steel is needed in making many things that we use every day of our lives. Among these products are:

. . . Cars, trucks, ships, and airplanes.

. . . Stoves, washing machines, and television sets.

. . . Heavy steel beams that are used to build skyscrapers and other large buildings.

Other metals. Many other kinds of metals are also produced by factories in the United States. Among the most important are copper, aluminum, lead, and zinc. These metals, too, are used in making a number of different products.

- How do you think your own life would be different if there were no metals such as iron and steel?
- What do you suppose would happen if our country ever ran out of the ores needed to make these metals? Is there much chance of this? Use your library to find out.

■ What natural resources are used for producing energy?

In every community, people need some form of energy to do work for them. Energy is needed to run machinery in factories and homes. It is also needed to move people and goods from place to place. Energy in the form of heat is needed to cook people's meals and to warm the air in houses and other buildings.

In the United States today, several different minerals are used to produce energy. The most important of these are coal, oil, and natural gas.

Coal. Coal is a soft black or brown rock that lies beneath the surface of the earth in many places. Sometimes people get coal by digging tunnels deep under the ground. At other times, they use the way shown on page 79. After the coal has been removed from the ground, it is loaded onto trucks or trains. These carry the coal to the places where it is needed.

More than half of the coal mined in our country is used by factories to produce electricity. Large amounts of coal are also made into a fuel called coke, which is needed for producing iron and steel. Factories also use coal in making many different kinds of chemicals.

Oil. Oil, or petroleum, is a liquid found in layers of rock or sand far beneath the ground. To get oil, people drill deep wells into the earth. The oil is pumped up or rises to the surface by itself. It is taken to factories called refineries. There it is made into gasoline, fuel oil, and other products. Gasoline is used as a fuel in cars, trucks, and tractors. Fuel oil is used to run trains and ships. It is also burned to heat buildings and to produce electric power. Chemicals made from petroleum are used in making hundreds of useful things, such as fertilizer, paint, medicines, and plastics.

Natural gas. Natural gas is another important resource. It is taken from the ground in much the same way as petroleum. Then it is sent through large pipes to homes and factories. In the United States, millions of people use natural gas to heat their houses. Natural gas is also used for cooking meals, heating water, drying laundry, and other purposes. Factories use large amounts of natural gas as a fuel. They also use it in making such things as phonograph records and automobile tires.

Waterpower. Not all of the energy used in our country comes from minerals. Some energy is supplied by the force of rushing water. Huge dams

A coal-mining machine. This huge machine removes soil and rock from the surface of the land. Then a power shovel digs up the coal that lies beneath the surface and loads it onto trucks. What is coal, and how was it formed? Use other books to help find the information you need.

like the one shown on pages 80 and 81 have been built across many rivers. These dams hold back the water to form large lakes. Some of the water stored in these lakes is allowed to flow through pipes inside

Drilling for oil. These men are working on a platform in the Pacific Ocean, off the coast of California. Why do you suppose people go out into the ocean to drill for oil?

Flaming Gorge Dam is on the Green River in the state of Utah. Who do you think built this dam? Give reasons for your answer. How does the dam help to produce electricity?

the dams. This rushing water helps to run machines that make electricity.

The energy shortage. In the last few years, people in the United States have been facing a problem known as the "energy shortage." Our country no longer has enough resources to meet all of its energy needs. To help meet these needs, it has bought large amounts of oil from other countries. But the cost of this oil has been rising rapidly. Also, there is a danger that some countries might decide not to sell us any more oil. Natural gas is also becoming hard to find and costly. Some experts believe that supplies of oil and natural gas may soon run out entirely. Although more and more coal is being mined, this resource will not last forever, either. And most of the rivers that are well suited for the making of electricity have already been dammed.

There are two main things that must be done to solve the energy problem. First, people must be careful not to use any more energy than they really need. For example, they can keep their houses cooler during the winter and drive smaller cars that use less gasoline. Second, people must try to find new ways of producing energy. Scientists are now looking for cheap and practical ways of using the energy contained in the sunlight. If they succeed, Americans may always have enough energy to meet their needs.

- What are some other ways of producing energy that may become important in the future? Look up "energy" in other books to find answers to this question.
- How can you and other members of your family save energy at home? List as many ways as you can.

■ How do Americans use their forest resources?

Forests cover about one third of the land in the United States. The trees that grow in these forests are a valuable natural resource.

Each year, workers called loggers cut down millions of trees in our country's forests. The logs are taken to factories, where they are used in many different ways. Much of the wood is sawed into lumber. This is used for building houses and making furniture. Some of the wood is made into a material called pulp. Paper and other things are made from this wood pulp. Wood is also used in making a number of useful chemicals.

Here are some other reasons why forests are important to Americans:

. . . Each year, millions of people come to the forests to enjoy camping, hiking, fishing, and other outdoor activities.

. . . Many kinds of wild animals live in the forests.

. . . Forests help us to conserve, or save, our soil and water resources.

Because forests are so valuable, they must be protected carefully. Enemies of the forests destroy millions of trees each year. One of these enemies is fire. (See pages 18-19.) Other important enemies are insects and diseases.

- In what ways do you think your life would be different if there were no forests?
- What is being done to protect our forests from enemies? To make sure that there will always be enough trees to meet our needs in the future? To answer these questions you will need to look in other books.

Unloading logs from a truck. What do you suppose will be done with these logs? Trees are an important natural resource in the United States. What are some of the reasons for this?

■ What resources are needed to produce our country's food?

Most of the food we eat comes from plants and animals that are raised on farms. In order to grow crops and raise livestock,* farmers need three main kinds of natural resources. These are sunshine, fresh water, and rich soil.

Many parts of the United States have all of these resources. Because of this, the United States is one of the most important farming countries in the world. Not only does it produce enough food to meet its own needs but it sells large amounts of food to other nations.

Some of the resources needed for producing food can be destroyed if they are not used carefully. For example, soil can be blown away by the wind or washed into rivers by heavy rains. Then the land will no longer be useful for growing crops. Farmers must learn the best ways to farm so that they will not waste any of their valuable resources.

- Does the place where you live have the natural resources needed for farming? Give facts to back up your answer.
- What resources besides sunshine, water, and soil do you think farmers might need to grow crops?

Fields of corn and hay in Wisconsin. Why are there strips of two different crops? Why are the rows curving instead of straight? Do you think the farmers here are using their natural resources wisely? Read about conservation* in other books to find answers to these questions.

The boys in this picture are helping to make a park for their neighborhood. What tools are they using? Would they be able to do this job without using any tools? Explain your answer.

8 Using Tools

■ How are tools used in everyday life?

If you have ever done any jobs around your home, you have probably used certain tools. For example, you may have used:

. . . A rake to pick up leaves.

. . . A shovel to clear the snow off your sidewalk.

. . . A wrench to tighten the handlebars on your bicycle.

. . . A hammer to pound nails into wood.

You have also used tools in school. Pens and pencils are tools. So are rulers, scissors, and erasers.

A tool is anything that people use to help them do work. There are many different kinds of tools. Some are very simple. For instance, a hammer is merely a piece of metal attached to a wooden handle. Other tools have many parts. The computers* shown in the picture on pages 2-3 have thousands of different parts.

Tools that have a number of moving parts are called machines. Today people use many different machines at home to help them do work. Among these machines are toasters, refrigerators, washers, vacuum cleaners, and lawnmowers. Machines such as typewriters and calculators* are often used in offices. Factories use machines to make hundreds of things we need and want in our everyday lives.

- How do tools help people meet their needs? Do you think people could meet their needs without using any tools? Explain.
- Would it be possible to have a community without tools? Give facts to support your answer.

■ What tools did the American Indians use?

The Indians who lived in North America long ago depended on certain kinds of tools to help them meet their needs. These tools seem quite simple compared to some of the machines that people use today. However, it took much skill and hard work to make them. The Indians did not have metals such as iron. Most of their tools were made of stone, wood, seashells, or animal bones.

The Indians used a number of different tools to get food. For example, hunters killed deer and other animals with bows and arrows, spears, and clubs. Fishers used spears, nets, or traps. Indian farmers dug holes with pointed sticks in order to plant seeds. They used hoes to dig up weeds, and

*See Glossary

sharp knives to harvest their crops. In some tribes, people ground corn in large wooden vessels to make cornmeal for bread. In other tribes, the kernels of corn were ground between large stones.

The Indians also used tools to make clothing and build homes. In many tribes, women sewed with needles made from animal bones or porcupine quills. Some Indians wove threads into cloth on a simple machine called a loom. Stone axes were sometimes used to cut down trees. Then stone wedges were used to split the logs into boards for making houses and furniture.

- How did the Indian hunters go about making their arrowheads and spearheads? Look in other books to find out more about the tools Indians used.

An Indian village along the Pacific Ocean, in what is now Washington State. One of the men in this picture is splitting logs into boards, which will be used to build a house. What tools is he using? How are these different from the tools people use to do the same job today?

■ What kinds of tools were used in the American colonies?

When settlers from Europe began coming to America in the 1600's, they brought many tools along with them. The Europeans knew how to make iron and other metals from ores. (See pages 74-75.) Metal tools were usually stronger and more useful than tools made from stone or wood.

The colonial farmers needed several kinds of tools to grow their crops. To prepare the soil for planting seeds, some farmers used heavy wooden plows that were pulled by horses or oxen. Other farmers used spades. Hoes were used to dig up weeds. To harvest the ripe grain, farmers used cradles* and other tools with sharp, curving blades. The grain was separated from the stalks by beating it with long wooden sticks called flails.

Afterwards the grain was ground into meal for making bread. In early days, people ground their grain by pounding it in wooden vessels much

A carpenter's shop in colonial times. What are the workers in this picture doing? What tools do you recognize? Are any of these tools like the ones used by Americans today? Explain.

Colonial farmers harvesting wheat. The man at the left is cutting the stalks of grain with a tool called a cradle. (Look up this word in the Glossary to find out how a cradle works.) The man at the right is raking up the stalks, while the man in the center is tying them into bundles. What changes have taken place in farming since colonial times?

like the ones used by the Indians. But as time passed, a number of grain mills were built in the colonies. A grain mill was usually located along a rushing stream. The flowing water turned a large wooden wheel. This wheel caused a heavy, flat stone called a millstone to turn round. As the millstone turned, it ground the kernels of grain into meal.

The colonists used many other tools in their work. For example:

. . . Hunters shot deer and other wild animals with guns.

. . . Loggers cut down trees with axes.

. . . Miners dug valuable ores out of the ground with picks and shovels.

. . . Blacksmiths used hammers and anvils* to pound red-hot pieces of iron into horseshoes.

. . . Carpenters used saws, hammers, and other tools to build houses and make furniture.

. . . Printers used machines called printing presses to make newspapers and books.

. . . Homemakers used brooms to sweep the floor and churns to make butter. They used spinning wheels to spin wool or flax into thread. Then they used looms to weave the thread into cloth.

- What are some ways in which life today is different from life in colonial times? Do these differences have anything to do with the kinds of tools that people use?

■ What was the Industrial Revolution?

In colonial times, there were no factories any-where in the world. Most people earned their living by farming. People who made cloth and other goods worked in their own homes or in small craft shops.

At that time, people knew only a few ways to supply energy* for doing work. Sometimes they used their own bodies to push, pull, lift, and carry different things. Sometimes they used animals to help them. Wind and flowing water provided energy for doing certain kinds of work. As you have seen, running water was sometimes used to grind grain. Sometimes windmills supplied the power to grind grain or to pump water.

About two hundred years ago, some important changes began taking place in England. Let us see what three of these changes were.

1. New machines were invented. During the 1700's, people in England invented new machines that were different from any that had been used before. These new machines could do many jobs that had always been done by hand. For example,

some machines were invented for spinning cotton into thread. Other machines could weave the thread into cloth.

2. <u>People began using steam power</u>. Much energy was needed to run the new machines. People wanted a way to provide more energy than they could get from wind or from flowing water.

An invention called the steam engine helped to meet this need. In a steam engine, coal or some other kind of fuel is burned to heat water. When the heated water turns to steam, pressure is built up. This pressure is used to supply the power needed to run machinery.

By using steam power, people could do much more work than they

An Englishman named Richard Arkwright invented a spinning machine in 1769. Arkwright's machine was run by waterpower. About this same time, people discovered a new way to provide energy for running machinery. What was this new source of energy, and how did it work?

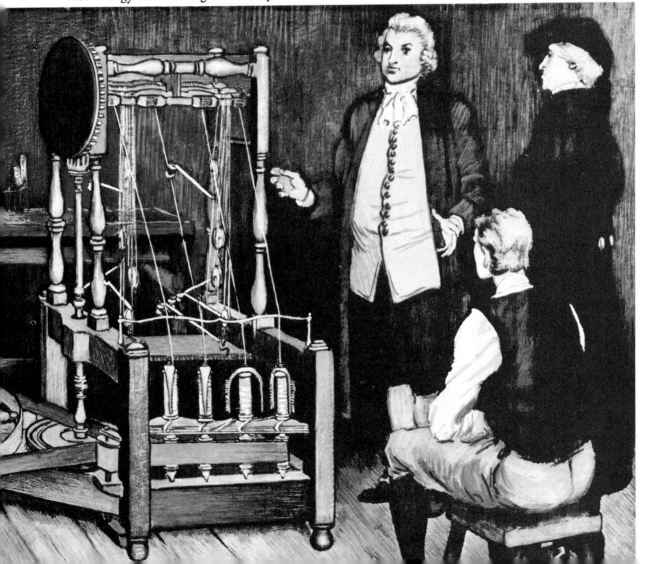

had been able to do by using wind power or waterpower. Steam engines were used to run the new spinning and weaving machines.

3. <u>Factories were built</u>. Most of the new machines were so large and needed so much power that they could not be placed in workers' homes. Instead, special buildings called factories were built. Workers were hired to come to the factories to run the new machines.

You have just read about three important changes that began to take place in people's ways of making goods. Together, these changes are known as the Industrial Revolution.

- Who was James Watt? What part did he play in the Industrial Revolution?
- How do you suppose the Industrial Revolution got its name? Look up the words "industry" and "revolution" in a dictionary to see if you can find the answer to this question.

A factory in England about one hundred years ago. Engines for ships were made in this building. In what ways was this early factory like a modern factory? In what ways was it different?

A **factory town in Pennsylvania** around the year 1900. Many of the people who lived in these houses worked in the nearby factories. Why do you suppose the houses were built so close to the factories?

■ How has the Industrial Revolution changed life in the United States?

The Industrial Revolution spread from England to other parts of the world. Among the first countries to start using the new ways of producing goods were Belgium, France, Germany, and the United States.

The United States was well suited to building factories. It was rich in coal, iron ore, wood, and other natural resources that were needed by industry. Rivers and streams provided large amounts of waterpower. In the United States, there were business people who had the money needed to build factories. There were also clever, skillful people who were able to invent new machines and new ways of doing things. Also, many people in the United States were eager to buy the goods that the new factories could produce.

As time passed, hundreds of factories were built in the United States. They brought great changes in people's ways of living. Many Americans left their farms and moved to cities and towns to take jobs in factories. By using the new machines, people were able to produce larger amounts of goods than ever before. They were also able to make many kinds of goods that could never have been made by hand.

- Why do you suppose so many Americans were willing to leave their farms and move to the cities to get jobs in factories? Do you think these people could meet their needs better by working in factories than they could by staying on their farms? Explain.

Today, important changes are still taking place in the ways that goods are made. Factories are using more and more machines that can do certain jobs almost entirely by themselves. The use of these new machines is called automation. Through automation, it is possible to run a whole factory with only a few highly trained workers.

- Do you think the United States could have become as large and powerful a nation as it is today without the help of modern machines? Why? Why not?
- In many countries of the world, the Industrial Revolution is just beginning. These countries have few factories. Most of the goods their people use are made with simple tools. Do you think these people can have as many goods to enjoy as people in countries that have many modern factories? Why do you think this way?

An automobile factory in Detroit, Michigan. What do you suppose is happening in this picture? Do you think we would be able to have automobiles without the help of modern machines? Explain your answer.

9 Division of Labor

■ How did Indian communities divide up their work?

The Indians in North America long ago needed many things. They had the same needs as all other people. (See pages 130-131.) They needed food, clothing, and shelter. Not all of the Indians met these needs in the same way.

The Indians who lived in the Eastern Woodlands* had several ways of getting food. The men spent much of their time hunting. They killed deer and other wild animals in the forests. They also fished in the lakes and streams. The women and children took care of small gardens. They raised corn, squash, and other crops. Sometimes they gathered food from trees and wild plants.

*See Glossary

The Hopi Indians lived in the Southwest.* They got most of their food by farming. How do you think these people divided up their work? Dividing up work among people who do different jobs is called division of labor. Does the picture below show any division of labor? Explain.

Huge herds of buffalo once lived on the Great Plains.* (See page 33.) Indians of the plains got food and other things they needed by hunting these animals. The men were the hunters. They went on long journeys looking for buffalo to kill. The women dried the buffalo meat for food. From the buffalo skins they made clothing. They also made the tepees in which they lived.

In the Southwest,* many Indians were farmers. They grew corn, beans, and other crops. The men did most of the work in the fields. The women prepared the food. They ground the corn into meal. They used the meal for making bread.

All Indian women had many other jobs. They made the clothing worn by their families. They made pottery, baskets, and other useful things. The women also took care of the young children.

The men usually ran the government of the tribe. They met and talked about important matters. They also made the laws for the tribe.

- How did the people in the Indian communities divide up their work? Give examples.
- What kinds of work did the men usually do? What kinds of work did the women usually do?
- Do you think men are always better than women at doing certain kinds of work? Do you think women are always better than men at doing other jobs?
- Do you think that the differences between the work that men and women do are caused mainly by what they were taught when they were children? Explain.
- Dividing up work among people who do different jobs is called division of labor. Do you think that the Indians of long ago had as much division of labor as we have today? Explain.

Blacksmiths at work in Williamsburg, Virginia. A blacksmith is a person who makes useful things from iron. In colonial days, every town had a blacksmith. Do you think blacksmiths spent part of their time growing crops? If not, how did they get the food they needed?

■ Did the American colonists use division of labor?

In the 1600's, settlers from Europe came to North America. They built small communities along the Atlantic coast. At first, life in these communities was very simple. Most families earned their living by farming. They grew or made nearly everything they needed. For example, the colonists made nearly all of their

own clothing and furniture. They also built their own houses.

Not all the people did exactly the same work. The men did most of the hard jobs in the fields. They plowed, planted, and harvested the crops. Women and children also helped out in the fields when the crops were ready to harvest. At that time of

year, many workers were needed. The men also did other hard jobs. For example, they built houses and barns.

The women of the colonies worked hard at many different jobs. They took care of the children and kept the house clean. They cooked the food and made most of the clothing for the family. They also made candles, soap, and other things the family needed.

In colonial days, women were not thought to be equal to men. They were not allowed to take part in the government. The men ran the community. They held meetings to choose government leaders. They also met to decide important matters.

As time passed, some of the farming communities grew into towns and cities. In these communities, not

Making candles by dipping string into a pot of hot, melted wax. Do you think men ever did this job in colonial days? Why? Why not?

all of the people were farmers. Some were soldiers or government workers. Others owned stores where people could buy goods. There were also people who worked at crafts. Blacksmiths made tools and other useful things from iron. There were also carpenters, weavers, and shoemakers.

These people did not meet all their needs by themselves. Instead, each person worked all day doing one job. With the money they earned, people could buy food and other things they needed.

- How did the colonists in farming communities divide up the work?
- What were some of the jobs in the early towns and cities? Do you think men and women did the same jobs? Why do you think this?
- Was it good to have some people work at jobs other than farming? Explain.

■ How does division of labor help Americans today?

Today, most people in the United States work at many different kinds of jobs. In other words, there is much division of labor.

Division of labor helps people to make more things than they could if each person worked alone. One reason for this is that every person can do some jobs better than other jobs. Also, every person likes to do some jobs better than others.

Think what would happen if you had to meet all of your needs by yourself. You would probably do some jobs well and other jobs poorly. But you would hardly ever spend enough time at a job to become really good at it.

When you spend all your time doing one kind of work, you can become very good at it. Also, you are happier doing a kind of work that you like. People who do only

San Francisco is a large city in California. More than three million people live in San Francisco and other communities nearby. What do you think are some of the jobs these people do? How does division of labor help the people of San Francisco?

Factory workers. About one fourth of all workers in our country have jobs in factories. Do you think that you would like to be a factory worker? Give reasons for your answer.

one kind of work can usually produce more than people who do many kinds of work.

Suppose, for example, that you enjoy working with numbers. You have a job as a bookkeeper in a business office. You are very good at your job. You have spent much time training for it. You would not like to work on a farm. You would not like to do some other kind of work where you cannot use your skills. On the other hand, the people who produce the things you buy could not do your job. And they probably would not enjoy doing it.

There is another reason why division of labor is helpful to communities. One person working alone could not make a machine such as an automobile or a computer.* Division of labor helps people to make many things that one person alone could not make. This is very important in a country like the United States. People here use many different kinds of machines.

- Do you have division of labor at your house? Explain. What would happen if your family did not divide up the work?
- Could we have the kinds of communities we have today without division of labor?
- Do you think that any other countries have as much division of labor as the United States does? Are there any countries that have very little division of labor? If so, which countries are they? Look in other books to find facts that will help answer these questions.

■ What kinds of jobs do people do today?

Nearly 220 million people live in the United States today. These people work at many different jobs. Some are farmers. They grow crops and raise animals such as cattle and hogs. Other people are miners. They dig coal, iron ore,* and other minerals* out of the earth. Still other people earn their living by fishing. Others cut down trees.

About one fourth of all workers in the United States today have jobs in factories. They make clothing, automobiles, radios, and other things that people want.

Millions of people work in stores where different kinds of goods are sold. Other workers have jobs in banks and business offices. Some people work for hotels, restaurants, and other businesses that serve travelers.

Many workers transport, or move, people and goods from one place to another. Among these workers are truck drivers, airplane pilots, and railroad engineers.

Office workers using a computer.* What does this picture tell you about division of labor?

Large numbers of people work in communications.* For example, many people work for telephone companies. Others work for companies that publish books, magazines, or newspapers. Still others have jobs with radio and television stations or motion picture studios.

Some people help build or repair houses and other buildings. These people include carpenters, plumbers, and painters. There are also workers who repair washers, dryers, and other machines that people use in their homes.

Many Americans provide services that people need. Among these workers are teachers, ministers, and lawyers. Barbers and beauty shop workers help people look neat. Doctors, dentists, and nurses help to take care of people's health needs.

A house painter. Do you think this man raises his own food and makes his own clothing? If not, how does he get the food and clothing he needs? Chapter 10 will help answer this question.

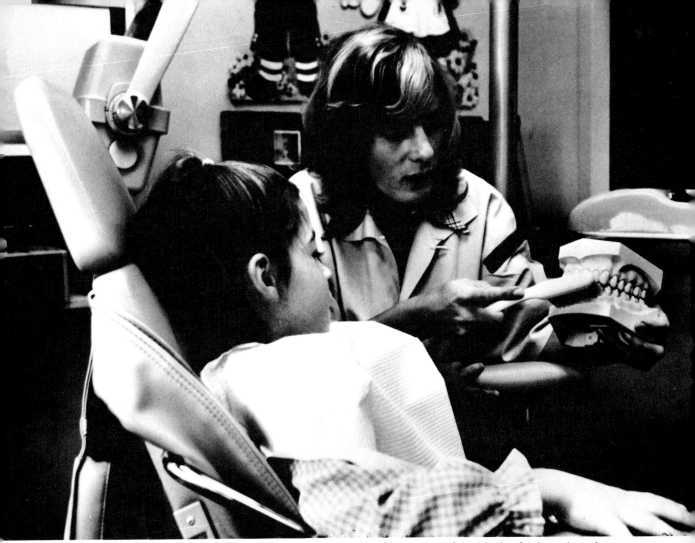

A dentist showing a girl the right way to brush her teeth. What kind of education do you think this woman needed to become a dentist? How do you suppose she got her education?

Millions of people in the United States work for the government. They perform many different tasks. For instance, police officers help to make sure that laws are obeyed. Fire fighters protect us from fires. Forest rangers watch over the trees in our forests. Health inspectors and garbage workers help to keep our cities clean and healthy. Soldiers and sailors guard our country against attack from enemy nations.

- Do you think that every kind of work is important to a community? Explain. How would we be able to meet our needs if people did not work at many different kinds of jobs?

- Do you think that most jobs today can be done equally well by men and women? Why? Why not? How has the division of labor between men and women changed since the early days of our country?

- Does every community need people who are well trained and willing to work hard at their jobs? Explain.

10 Exchange

■ How did the pioneers use the great idea of exchange?

About two hundred years ago, pioneers from the eastern part of our country began moving west of the Appalachian Mountains.* At that time, the land between the Appalachians and the Mississippi River was covered with thick forests. The pioneers cut down some of the trees in these forests so they could use the land for farming.

Life was hard for the pioneers who lived on the western frontier. These people had to make or grow almost everything they needed. They seldom bought goods in stores. But they sometimes exchanged goods with each other to get things they needed. Suppose a farmer grew more corn than his family could use. He might give the extra corn to a neighbor in exchange for a pair of shoes. Exchange helped the pioneers to meet their needs for food, clothing, and shelter.

Before long, the pioneers were raising more crops than they needed for their own use. They began to sell some of their crops to people in the eastern part of the United States. The pioneers received money in exchange for their crops. With this money, they could buy goods that they were not able to make or grow themselves.

In those days, there were no railroads or good roads along the western frontier. The easiest way to send goods from one place to another was by boat. The pioneers would load their corn, lumber, and other products onto flatboats.* They would float these boats down the Mississippi River to the city of New Orleans. There, sailing ships would pick up the goods and carry them to cities along the eastern coast of our country.

As time passed, more people came to the lands west of the Appalachian Mountains. Towns and cities began

*See Glossary

A pioneer village in Ohio. This picture shows a farmer bringing some grain to the mill to be ground into flour. The farmer will give the miller some of the flour to pay him for grinding the grain. Do you think the farmer is carrying on exchange? Explain your answer.

to grow up there. Farmers came to the towns to sell their crops. In the towns, they also bought some of the things they needed.

People who lived in the pioneer towns worked at many different kinds of jobs. For instance, some were carpenters, blacksmiths, or millers. Others were storekeepers. Still others were doctors, lawyers, or teachers.

- Do you think that the pioneer farmers had much division of labor? Explain. (Before you answer, you may want to read Chapter 9 again.)

- How did exchange help the pioneers meet their needs?

- Was there more division of labor in the towns and cities than there was on the pioneer farms? Did people there have more need to exchange goods with each other? Give facts to back up your answers.

■ How do Americans today meet their needs through exchange?

Today, most Americans have a way of life that is very different from that of the pioneers. They no longer grow or make most of the things they need by themselves. Instead, they obtain these goods through exchange with other people.

How money is used for exchange. Sometimes people still exchange goods directly with one another. For instance, you might give some fish you have just caught to a friend in exchange for some tomatoes that were grown in your friend's garden. This kind of exchange is known as barter.

Today, however, people do not usually get the things they need through barter. Instead, they use money to carry on exchange. When people work at jobs, they receive money in exchange for their labor. They can then exchange this money for the goods and services they need.

Shoppers in a supermarket. Are these people carrying on exchange? What makes you think this? Where do you suppose the goods in this store came from? How do you think they were brought to the store? You may want to do some reading in other books to find the answers.

A family eating dinner. What things in the picture do you think these people might have grown or made themselves? What things do you think they bought in stores? Could the members of this family meet most of their needs without using exchange? Explain your answer.

Money makes it easier for people to carry on exchange. To understand why this is true, imagine that you live in a place where money is not used. You earn your living as a baker. Each day, you make bread, cakes, and other things for people to eat. Suppose that you need a new pair of shoes. You must find someone who can make the kind of shoes you want. At the same time, this person must be willing to take some of your baked goods in exchange for the shoes. Then you will have to decide how many loaves of bread a pair of shoes is worth. You can see why most people would rather use money instead of barter to get the things they need.

Retail and wholesale trade. In our country today, there are millions of stores where people can buy goods. Some of these stores are very large. Others are very small. Stores that sell goods directly to the people who will use them are called <u>retail</u> stores.

Where do the retail stores get the goods they sell? Sometimes they buy these goods directly from the factories or farms where they are produced. Sometimes other companies buy the goods from farms and factories, and then sell them to the retail stores. These companies are said to be carrying on <u>wholesale</u> trade.

- Do you think it would be possible to have division of labor without exchange? Explain your answer.
- In some parts of the world today, people still use barter instead of money. Do you think you would like to use this way of carrying on exchange? Why? Why not?
- What would happen to a community if people could not carry on exchange with each other?

■ **Why do people in different communities or countries trade with each other?**

Trade between communities. We have seen that exchange, or trade, is carried on between the people of a community. Trade also takes place between people in different communities.

There are several reasons why trade between different communities is important. Sometimes facto-

ries in one city are better able to make a certain product than factories in another city. Or the people of one community are more skillful at making a certain product than the people of another community.

Some parts of a country have certain natural resources that other parts do not have. For example, in the state of Utah the climate is not good for growing oranges. But Utah has large deposits of copper. This metal is used in making wire and many other kinds of products. The

state of Florida does not have any large deposits of copper. However, the climate in some parts of Florida is very good for growing oranges. Florida can ship some of its oranges to Utah. It can buy copper from Utah in exchange. Through trade, people in both Florida and Utah can get things that they would not be able to produce themselves.

Trade between countries. Exchange is also carried on between the people of different nations. The reasons for this trade are the same as those for trade between different communities. For example, the United States does not have the right kind of climate for growing bananas. However, it does have many large automobile factories. Ecuador, a country

A jet airplane that carries goods between cities in different parts of the United States. Do you think that exchange is important to every community? Give reasons for your answer.

Workers loading goods on a ship at New Orleans, Louisiana. The ship will carry these goods to countries in South America. Why do different countries need to trade with each other?

in South America, does not have any automobile factories. But the climate there is very good for growing bananas. The United States can sell cars to Ecuador and buy bananas in exchange. This helps the people of both countries. They can enjoy goods that they would not have at all if there were no trade.

- What goods does your family get from other communities in your state? What goods does it get from other states in your country? From other countries?
- "Through trade, all people on earth can have a better life." Do you agree with this statement? Why? Why not?

SKILLS MANUAL

CONTENTS

Thinking

One of the main reasons you are attending school is to learn how to think clearly. Your social studies class is one of the best places in which to grow in the use of your thinking skills. Here you will learn more about using the thinking skills that will help you understand yourself, your country, and your world.

There are seven different kinds of thinking skills. As you use all seven, you will become more successful in school and in life. You will be able to understand yourself and your world much better. You will be a happier and more useful citizen as well.

Seven kinds of thinking

1. **Remembering** is the simplest kind of thinking. Everything you can remember is called your store of knowledge.

   Example: Remembering facts, such as the names of state capitals.

2. **Translation** is changing information from one form into another.

   Example: Reading a map and putting into words the information you find there.

3. **Interpretation** is discovering how things relate to each other, or how things are connected.

   Example: Comparing two pictures to decide in what ways they are alike or in what ways they are different.

4. **Application** is using your knowledge and skills to solve a new problem.

   Example: Using social studies skills to prepare a written report.

5. **Analysis** is the kind of thinking you use when you try to find out how something is organized, or put together. When you

use this kind of thinking, you separate complicated information into its basic parts. Then you can see how they were put together and how they are related to each other.

Example: Separating main ideas from supporting facts.

6. **Synthesis** is putting ideas together in a form that not only has meaning but is also new and original.

Examples: Painting a picture; or writing something original, which might be a paragraph or an entire poem, story, or play.

7. **Evaluation** is the highest level of thinking. It is judging whether or not something meets a given standard.

Example: Deciding which of several different sources of information is the most reliable; or judging the success of a class discussion.

Solving Problems

The social studies will be more worthwhile to you if you learn to think and work as a scientist does. Scientists use a special way of studying called the problem-solving method. During the 1900's, the use of this method has helped people gain much scientific knowledge. In fact, we have gained more scientific knowledge during the 1900's than people had discovered earlier throughout the history of human beings on this planet.

The problem-solving method is more interesting than simply reading a textbook and memorizing answers for a test. By using this method, you can make your own discoveries. Using the problem-solving method will also help you learn how to think clearly. It will involve you in using all of the seven different kinds of thinking skills. To use this method in learning about our country, you will need to follow these steps.

1. **Choose an important, interesting problem** that you would like to solve. (A sample problem to solve is given on the opposite page.) Write the problem down so that you will have clearly in mind what it is you want to find out. If there are small problems that need to be solved in order to solve your big problem, list them, too.

2. **Think about all possible solutions** to your problem. List the ones that seem most likely to be true. These possible solutions are called "educated guesses," or hypotheses. You will try to solve your problem by finding facts to support or to disprove your hypotheses.

Sometimes you may wish to do some general background reading before you make your hypotheses. For example, if you were going to solve the sample problem on the opposite page, you might want first to read about the land features of the Northeast. Then, make your hypotheses based on what you have discovered.

3. **Test your hypotheses** by doing research. This book provides you with four major sources of information. These are the pictures, the text, the maps, and the Glossary. To find the information you need, you may use the Table of Contents and the Index. The suggestions on pages 116-119 will help you find and evaluate other sources of information.

As you do research, make notes of all the information that will either support your hypotheses or disprove them. You may discover that information from one source does not agree with information from another. If this should happen, check still further. Try to decide which facts are correct.

4. **Summarize what you have learned.** Your summary should be a short statement of the main points you have discovered. Have you been able to support one or more of your hypotheses with facts? Have you been able to prove that one or more of your hypotheses is not correct? What new facts have you learned? Do you need to do more research?

You may want to write a report about the problem. To help other people share the ideas you have come to understand, you may decide to include maps, pictures, or your own drawings with your report. You will find helpful suggestions for writing a good report on pages 119 and 120.

A sample problem to solve

As you study our country, you may wish to try to solve problems about our country as a whole. Or, you may wish to study one major region. The following sample problem to solve is about the Northeast as a region.

Mountains and rolling hills make up much of the Northeast. Very little of this part of our country is low and level. How do the land features of the Northeast affect the lives of the people? In forming hypotheses to solve this problem, you will need to think about how the land features of the Northeast affect the following:

a. where the cities grew up
b. industry
c. farming

The suggestions on the next two pages will help you find the information you need for solving this problem.

Learning Social Studies Skills

What is a skill?

A skill is something that you have learned to do well. To learn some skills, such as swimming or playing baseball, you must train the muscles of your arms and legs. To learn others, such as typing, you must train your fingers. Still other skills call for you to train your mind. For instance, reading with understanding is a skill that calls for much mental training. The skills that you use in the social studies are largely mental skills.

Why are skills important?

Mastering different skills will help you to have a happier and more satisfying life. You will be healthier and enjoy your free time more if you develop skills needed to take part in different sports. By developing art and music skills, you will be able to share your feelings more fully. It is even more important for you to develop your mental skills. These skills are the tools that you will use in getting and using the knowledge you need to live successfully in today's world.

Developing a skill

If you were to ask fine athletes or musicians how they gained their skills, they would probably say, "Through practice."

To develop mental skills, you must practice also. Remember, however, that a person cannot become a good ballplayer if he or she keeps throwing the ball in the wrong way. A person cannot become a fine musician by practicing the wrong notes. The same thing is true of mental skills. To master them, you must practice them correctly.

The following pages have suggestions about how to perform correctly several important skills needed in the social studies. For example, to succeed in the social studies you must know how to find the information you need. You need to know how to prepare reports and how to work with others on group projects. Study these skills carefully, and use them.

How To Find Information You Need

Each day of your life you seek information. Sometimes you want to know certain facts just because you are curious. Most of the time, however, you want information for some certain reason. If you enjoy baseball, for instance, you may want to know how to figure batting averages. If you collect stamps, you need to know how to find out what countries they come from. As a student in today's world, you need information for many reasons. As an adult, you will need even more knowledge in order to live successfully in tomorrow's world.

You may wonder how you can possibly learn all the facts you are going to need during your lifetime. The answer is that you can't. Therefore, knowing how to find information when you need it is very important to you. Following are suggestions for finding good sources of information and for using these sources to find the facts that you need.

Written Sources of Information

Books

You may be able to find the information you need in books that you have at home or in your classroom. To see if a textbook or other nonfiction* book has the information you need, look at the table of contents and the index.

Sometimes, you will need to go to your school or neighborhood library to find books that have the information you want. To make the best use of a library, you should learn to use the card catalog. This is a file that contains information about the books in the library. Each nonfiction book has at least three cards, filed in alphabetical order. One is for the title, one is for the author, and one is for the subject of the book. Each card gives the book's special number. This number will help you to find the book. All the nonfiction books in the library are arranged on the shelves in numerical order. If you cannot find a book that you want, the librarian will help you.

Reference volumes

You will find much useful information in certain books known as reference volumes. Among these are dictionaries, encyclopedias, atlases, and other special books. Some companies publish a book each year with facts and figures and general information about the events of the year before. Such books are generally called yearbooks, annuals, or almanacs.

Newspapers and magazines

These are important sources of up-to-date information. Sometimes you will want to look for information in papers or magazines that you do not have at home. You can almost always find the ones you want at the library.

The *Readers' Guide to Periodical Literature* is kept for use in most libraries. It will direct you to magazine articles about the subject you are interested in. This is a series of volumes that list articles by title, author, and subject. In the front of each volume is an explanation of the abbreviations used to indicate the different magazines and their dates.

Booklets, pamphlets, and bulletins

You can get many materials of this kind from local and state governments, as well as from our federal government. Chambers of commerce, travel bureaus, trade organizations, private companies, and embassies of other countries publish materials that have a wealth of information.

Many booklets and bulletins give correct information. Remember, however, that some of them were written to promote certain goods or ideas. Information from such sources should be checked carefully.

*See Glossary

Reading for Information

The following suggestions will help you to save time and work when you are looking for information in books and other written materials.

The table of contents and the index

The table of contents appears at the beginning of the book and generally is a list of the chapters in the book. By looking at this list, you can almost always tell if the book has the kind of information you need.

The index is a more detailed list of the things that are talked about in the book. It will help you find the pages on which specific facts are talked about. In most books, the index is at the back. Encyclopedias often place the index in a separate volume.

At the beginning of an index, you will generally find an explanation that makes it easier to use. For instance, the beginning of the Index for this book tells you that *p* means picture and *m* means map.

The topics, or entries, in the index are arranged in alphabetical order. To find all the information you need, you may have to look under more than one entry. For example, to find out what pages of a social studies book have information about cities, you would look up the entry for cities. You could also see if cities are listed by their own names.

Skim the written material

Before you begin reading a chapter or a page, skim it to see if it has the information you need. In this way you will not waste time reading something that is of little or no value to you. When you skim, you look mainly for topic headings, topic sentences, and key words. Imagine you are looking for the answer to the question: "What are the people in the West doing to conserve their forest resources?" In a book about the West or about the United States, you might look for a topic heading that mentions forest resources. When you find this heading, you might look for the key words, "conserving forests."

Read carefully

When you think you have found the page that has the information you are looking for, read it carefully. Does this page tell you exactly what you want to know? If not, you will need to look further.

Other Ways of Getting Information

Direct experience

What you see or live through for yourself may be a good source of information if you have watched carefully and remembered accurately. Firsthand information can often be obtained by visiting places in your community or nearby, such as museums, factories, or government offices.

Radio and television

Use the listings in your local newspaper to find programs about the subjects in which you are interested.

Movies, filmstrips, recordings, and slides

Materials on many different subjects are available. You can get them from schools, libraries, museums, and private companies.

Resource people

Sometimes, you will be able to get information by talking with a person who has special knowledge. Once in a while, you may wish to invite someone to speak to your class and answer questions.

Evaluating Information

During your lifetime, you will constantly need to evaluate what you see, hear, and read. Information is not true or worthwhile simply because it is presented on television or is written in a book, magazine, or newspaper. The following suggestions will help you in evaluating information.

Primary and secondary sources of information

A primary source of information is a firsthand record. For instance, a photograph taken of something while it is happening is a primary source. So is the report you write about a field trip you take. Original documents, such as the Constitution of the United States, are primary sources also.

A secondary source is a secondhand report. If you write a report about what someone else told you he or she saw, your report will be a secondary source of information. Another example of a secondary source is a history book.

Advanced scholars like to use primary sources whenever possible. However, these sources are often difficult to obtain. Most students in elementary and high school use secondary sources. You should always be aware that you are using secondhand information when you use a secondary source.

Who said it and when was it said?

The next step in evaluating information is to ask, "Who said it?" Was she a person with special training in the subject about which she wrote? Was he a newsman who is known for careful reporting of the facts?

Another question you should ask is "When was it said?" Changes take place rapidly in our world, and the information you are using may be out of date. For instance, suppose you are looking for information about a country. If you use an encyclopedia that is five years old, much of the information you find will not be correct.

Is it mostly fact or opinion?

The next step in evaluating information is to decide if it is based on facts or if it consists mostly of unsupported opinions. You can do this best if you know about these three kinds of statements:

1. Statements of fact that can be checked. For example, "Voters in the United States choose their representatives by secret ballot" is a statement of fact that can be checked by finding out how voting is carried on in different parts of our country.

2. Inferences, or conclusions that are based on facts. The statement "The people of the United States live in a democracy" is an inference. This inference is based on the fact that the citizens choose their representatives by secret ballot, and on other facts that can be proved. It is important to remember that inferences can be false or only partly true, even though they are based on facts.

3. Value judgments, or opinions. The statement "It is always wrong for a country to go to war" is a value judgment. Since a value judgment is an opinion, you need to look at it very carefully. On what facts and inferences is it based? What facts and conclusions do you think form the basis of the opinion, "It is always wrong for a country to go to war"? Do you agree or disagree with these conclusions? Trustworthy writers or reporters are careful to let their readers know which statements are their own opinions. They also try to base their opinions as much as possible on facts that can be proved.

Why was it said?

The next step in evaluating information is to find out the purpose for which it was prepared. Many books and articles are prepared in an honest effort to give you accurate information. Scientists writing about new scientific discoveries will generally try to report their findings as accurately as possible. They will be careful to distinguish between things they have actually seen and conclusions they have drawn from their observations.

Some information, however, is prepared mostly to persuade people to believe or act a certain way. Information of this kind is called propaganda.

Some propaganda is used to promote causes that are generally thought to be good. A picture that shows Smokey the Bear and the words "Only you can prevent forest fires" is an example of this kind of propaganda.

Propaganda is also used to make people support causes they would not agree with if they knew more about them. This kind of propaganda may be made up of information that is true, partly true, or false. Even when it is true, however, the information may be presented in such a way as to mislead you.

Propaganda generally appeals to people's feelings rather than to their thinking ability. For this reason, you should learn to recognize information that is propaganda. Then you can think about it calmly and clearly, and evaluate it intelligently.

Making Reports

There are many times when you need to share information or ideas with others. Sometimes you will need to do this in writing. Other times you will need to do it by speaking. One of the best ways to develop your writing and speaking skills is by making written and oral reports. The success of your report will depend on how well you have organized your material. It will also depend on your skill in presenting it. Here are some guidelines that will help you in preparing a good report.

Decide upon a goal

Have your goal clearly in mind. Are you mostly interested in sharing information? Do you want to give your own ideas on a subject? Or are you trying to persuade other people to agree with you?

Find the information you need

Be sure to use more than one source. If you are not sure how to find information about your subject, read the suggestions on pages 116 and 117.

Take good notes

To remember what you have read, you must take notes. Before you begin taking notes, however, you will need to make a list of the questions you want your report to answer. As you do research, write down the facts that answer these questions. You may find some interesting and important facts that do not answer any of your questions. If you feel that they might be useful in your report, write them down, too. Your notes should be short and in your own words except when you want to use quotations. When you use an exact quotation, be sure to put quotation marks around it.

You will be able to make the best use of your notes if you write them on file cards. Use a separate card for each statement or group of statements that answers one of your questions. To remember where your information came from, write on each card the title, author, and date of the source. When you have finished taking notes, group the cards according to the questions they answer.

Make an outline

After you have reviewed your notes, make an outline. This is a general plan that shows the order and the relationship of the ideas you want to include in your report. The first step in making an outline is to pick out the main ideas. These will be the main headings in your outline. (See sample outline below.) Next, list under each of these headings the ideas and facts that support or explain it. These related ideas are called subheadings. As you arrange your information, ask yourself the following questions.

a. Is there one main idea I must put first because everything else depends on this idea?
b. Have I arranged my facts in such a way as to show relationships among them?

c. Are there some ideas that will be clearer if they come after other ideas have been explained?

d. Have I included enough facts so that I can end my outline with a summary statement or a logical conclusion?

When you have finished your first outline, you may find that some parts of it are too short. If so, you may wish to do more research. When you feel that you have enough information, make your final outline. Remember that this outline will serve as a guide for your finished report.

Example of an outline

The author of this Skills Manual prepared the following outline before writing "Making Reports."

I. Introduction
II. Deciding upon a goal
III. Finding information
IV. Taking notes
   A. List main ideas to be researched
   B. Write on file cards facts that support or explain these ideas
   C. Group cards according to main ideas
V. Making an outline
   A. Purpose of an outline
   B. Guidelines for arranging information
   C. Sample outline of this section
VI. Preparing a written report
VII. Presenting an oral report

Special guidelines for a written report

Using your outline as a guide, write your report. The following suggestions will help you to make your report interesting and clear.

Create word pictures that your readers can see in their minds. Before you begin, imagine that you are going to make a movie of the subject you plan to write about. What scenes would you like to show? Next, think of the words that will bring these same pictures into your readers' minds.

Group your sentences into good paragraphs. It is generally best to begin a paragraph with a topic sentence that says to the reader, "This is what you will learn about in this paragraph." The other sentences in the paragraph should help to support or explain the topic sentence.

A sample paragraph. Below is a sample paragraph from a textbook about the northeastern part of our country. The topic sentence has been underlined. Notice how clear it is and how well the other sentences support it. Also notice how many pictures the paragraph puts in your mind.

One of the most interesting sights in the Erie-Ontario Lowland is beautiful Niagara Falls. These falls are located on the Niagara River, which forms part of the border between the United States and Canada. The Niagara River flows northward from Lake Erie to Lake Ontario. About halfway between these two lakes, the river plunges over a steep cliff, forming Niagara Falls. Each year, thousands of tourists come to see these famous falls. Waterpower from the falls is used to produce electricity for factories and homes in both the United States and Canada.

Other guidelines. There are two other things to remember in writing a good report. First, use the dictionary to find the spelling of words you are not sure about. Second, make a list of the sources of information you used. Put this list at the beginning or end of your report. This list is called a bibliography.

Special guidelines for an oral report

When you are going to give a report orally, you will also want to arrange your information in a logical order by making an outline. Prepare notes to guide you during your talk. These notes should be complete enough to help you remember all the points you want to make. You may even write out certain parts of your report that you would rather read.

When you present your report, speak directly to your audience. Pronounce your words correctly and clearly. Remember to speak slowly enough for your listeners to follow what you are saying. Use a tone of voice that will hold their interest. Stand up straight, but try not to be too stiff. Remember, the only way to improve your speaking skills is to practice them correctly.

Holding a Group Discussion

One of the important ways in which you learn is by exchanging ideas with other people. You do this often in everyday conversation. You are likely to learn more, however, when you take part in the special kind of group conversation that we call a discussion. A discussion is more orderly than a conversation. It generally has a definite, serious purpose. This purpose may be the sharing of information or the solving of a problem. In order to reach its goal, the discussion group must arrive at a conclusion or make a decision of some kind.

The guidelines below will help you to have a successful discussion.

Be prepared

Think about the subject to be discussed ahead of time. Prepare for the discussion by reading and taking notes. You may also want to make an outline of the ideas you want to share with the group.

Take part

Take part in the discussion. Express your ideas clearly and in as few words as possible. Be sure that the statements you make and the questions you ask deal with the subject being talked about.

Listen and think

Listen thoughtfully to others. Encourage all of the members of the discussion group to express their ideas. Do not make up your mind about a question or a problem until all of the facts have been given.

Be courteous

When you speak, address the whole group. Ask and answer questions politely. When you do not agree with someone, give your reasons in a friendly way.

Working With Others

In school and throughout life, you will find that there are many things that can be done better by a group than by one person working alone. Some of these projects would take too long to finish if they were done by one person. Others have different parts that can be done best by people with different talents.

Before your group begins a project, you should decide several matters. First, decide exactly what goal you are trying to reach. Second, decide what part of the project each person should do. Third, decide when the project is to be finished.

Do your part

Remember that the success of your project depends on every member of the group. Be willing to do your share of the work and to accept your share of the responsibility.

Follow the rules

Help the group decide on reasonable rules. Then follow them. When a difference of opinion cannot be settled by discussion, make a decision by majority* vote.

Share your ideas

Be willing to share your ideas with the group. When you present an idea for discussion, be prepared to see it criticized or even rejected. At the same time, have the courage to stand up for an idea or a belief that is really important to you.

Be friendly, thoughtful, helpful, cheerful

Try to express your opinions seriously and sincerely without hurting others or losing their respect. Listen politely to the ideas of others.

Learn from your mistakes

Look for ways in which you can be a better group member the next time you work with others on a project.

Building Your Vocabulary

When you do research in many different kinds of reading materials, you are likely to find several words you have never seen before. If you skip over these words, you may not fully understand what you are reading. The following suggestions will help you to discover the meanings of new words and build your vocabulary.

1. See how the word is used in the sentence. When you come to a new word, don't stop reading. Read on beyond the new word to see if you can discover any hints as to what its meaning might be. Trying to figure out the meaning of a word from the way it is used may not give you the exact definition. However, it will give you a general idea of what the word means.

2. Sound out the word. Break the word up into syllables, and try to pronounce it. When you say the word aloud, you may find that you know it after all but have simply never seen it in print.

3. Look in the dictionary. When you think you have figured out what a word means and how it is pronounced, look it up in the dictionary. First, check the pronunciation. Have you pronounced it correctly? Then, check the meaning of the word. Remember, most words have more than one meaning. Did you decide on the right definition?

4. Make a list of the new words you learn. In your own words, write a definition of each word you place on your list. Review this list from time to time.

Learning Map Skills

The earth is a sphere

Our earth is round like a ball. We call anything with this shape a sphere. The earth is, of course, a very large sphere. Its diameter* is about 8,000 miles (12,874 kilometers*). Its circumference* is about 25,000 miles (40,233 kilometers). The earth is not quite a perfect sphere. It is somewhat flat at the North and South poles.

Globes and maps

The globe in your classroom is also a sphere. It is a small-size copy of the earth. The surface of the globe shows the shapes of the areas of land on the earth. It also shows the shapes of the different bodies of water. By looking at the globe, you can see exactly where the continents,* islands, and oceans are. Globes are made with the North Pole at the top. But they are often tipped to show the way the earth is tipped. Maps are flat drawings. They may show part or all of the earth's surface.

Scale

Globes and maps give information about distance. When you use them, you need to know what distance on the earth is represented by a given distance on the globe or map. This relationship is called the scale. The scale of a globe or map may be shown in several different ways.

On most maps, the scale is shown by a small drawing. For example:

Scale

0	200	400 Miles
0	322	644 Kilometers

Sometimes, the scale is shown in this way: 1 inch = 400 miles (644 kilometers).

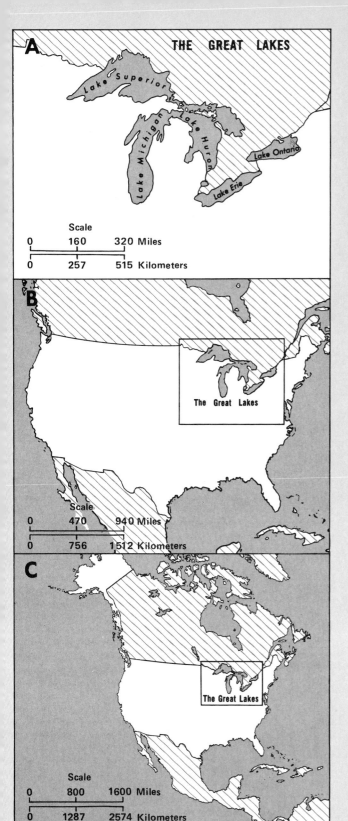

A

Lake Superior
Lake Michigan
Lake Huron
Lake Erie
Lake Ontario

Scale
0   160   320 Miles
0   257   515 Kilometers

B

The Great Lakes

Scale
0   470   940 Miles
0   756   1512 Kilometers

C

The Great Lakes

Scale
0   800   1600 Miles
0   1287   2574 Kilometers

The **Great Lakes area** is a different size on each of the three maps above. This is because one inch on each of these maps represents a different distance on the earth.

Finding places on the earth

Map makers, travelers, and other interested people have always wanted to know just where certain places are. Over the years, a very accurate way of giving such information has been worked out. This system is used all over the world.

In order to work out a means of finding anything, you need starting points and a measuring unit. The North and South poles and the equator are the starting points for the system we use to find places on the earth. The measuring unit for our system is called the degree ($^\circ$).

Parallels show latitude

When we want to find a place on the earth, we first find out how far it is north or south of the equator. This distance measured in degrees is called north or south latitude. The equator stands for zero latitude. The North Pole is located at 90 degrees north latitude. The South Pole is at 90 degrees south latitude.

All points on the earth that have the same latitude are the same distance from the equator. A line connecting such points is called a parallel. This is because it is parallel to the equator. (See globe D on the next page.)

Meridians show longitude

After we know the latitude of a place, we need to know its location in an east-west direction. This is called its longitude. The lines that show longitude are called meridians. They are drawn so as to connect the North and South poles (See globe E on the next page.) Longitude is measured from the meridian that passes through Greenwich, England. This line of zero longitude is called the prime meridian. Distance east or west of this meridian measured in degrees is called east or west longitude. The meridian of 180 degrees west longitude is the same as the one of 180 degrees east longitude. This is because 180 degrees is exactly halfway around the world.

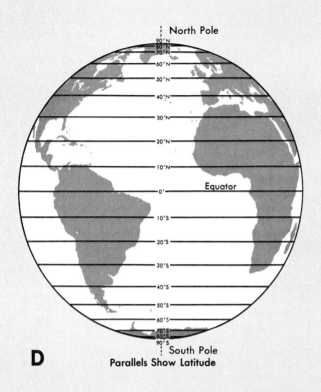

D
Parallels Show Latitude

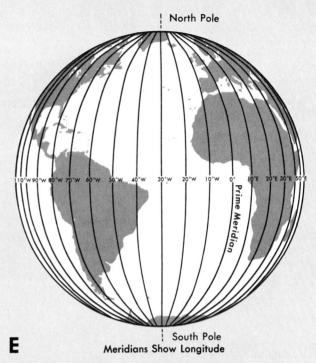

E
Meridians Show Longitude

Finding places on a globe

The location of a certain place might be given to you like this: 30° N 90° W. This means that this place is located 30 degrees north of the equator, and 90 degrees west of the prime meridian. See if you can find this place on the globe in your classroom. It is helpful to remember that parallels and meridians are drawn every ten or fifteen degrees on most globes.

The round earth on a flat map

An important fact about a sphere is that you cannot flatten out its surface perfectly. To prove this, you might do the following. Cut an orange in half. Scrape away the fruit. You will not be able to press either piece of orange peel flat without crushing it. If you cut one piece in half, however, you can press these smaller pieces nearly flat. Next, cut one of these pieces of peel into three smaller pieces, shaped like those in drawing F on the opposite page. You will be able to press these pieces quite flat.

A map like the one shown in drawing F can be made by cutting the surface of a globe into twelve pieces shaped like the smallest pieces of your orange peel. Such a map would be accurate. However, an "orange-peel" map is not easy to use, because the continents and oceans are cut apart.

A flat map can never show the earth's surface as truthfully as a globe can. On globes, shape, size, distance, and direction are all accurate. A single flat map of the world cannot be drawn to show all four of these things correctly. But flat maps can be made that show some of these things accurately. The different ways of drawing maps of the world to show different things correctly are called map projections.

The Mercator projection

Drawing G, on the opposite page, shows a world map called a Mercator projection. When you compare this map with a globe, you can see that continents, islands, and oceans have almost the right shape. On this kind of map, however, North America seems larger than Africa. This is not true. On Mercator maps, lands far from the equator appear larger than they are.

Because they show true directions, Mercator maps are very useful to sailors and fliers. For instance, the city of Lisbon, Portugal, lies almost exactly east of Baltimore, Maryland. A Mercator map shows that a ship could reach Lisbon by sailing from Baltimore straight east across the Atlantic Ocean. A plane could also reach Lisbon by flying straight east from Baltimore.

The shortest route

Strangely enough, the best way to reach Lisbon from Baltimore is not by going straight east. There is a shorter route. In order to understand why this is so, you might like to do the following.

On your classroom globe, find Lisbon and Baltimore. Both cities lie just south of the 40th parallel. Take a piece of string and connect the two cities. Let the string follow the true east-west direction of the 40th parallel. Now, draw the string tight. Notice that it passes far to the north of the 40th parallel. The path of the tightened string is the shortest route between Baltimore and Lisbon. The shortest route between any two points on the earth is called the great* circle route.

A Round Globe on a Flat Surface

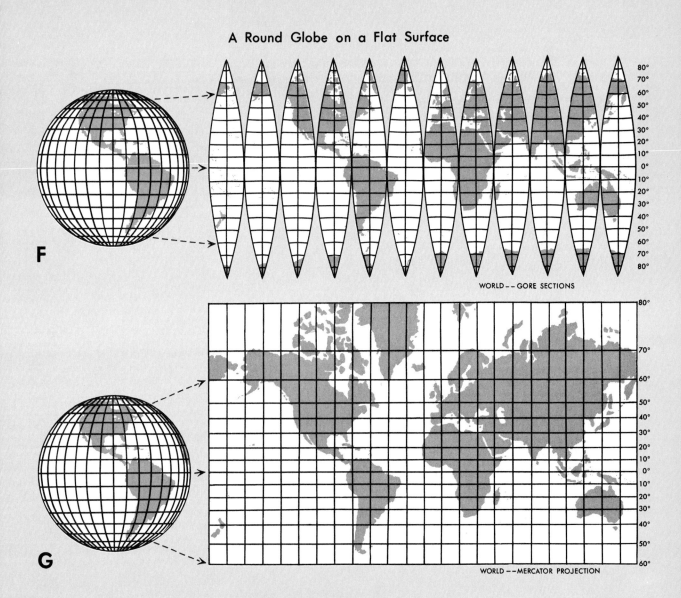

F

WORLD -- GORE SECTIONS

G

WORLD -- MERCATOR PROJECTION

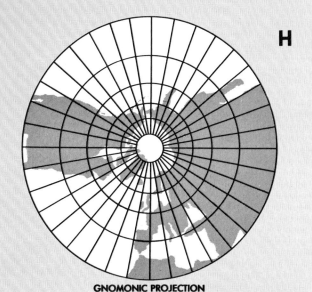

H

GNOMONIC PROJECTION

The gnomonic (nō mon′ik) projection

Using a globe and a piece of string is not a very handy or accurate way of finding great circle routes. Instead, sailors and fliers use a special kind of map called the gnomonic projection. (See drawing H, at left.) On this kind of map, the great circle route between any two places can be found simply by drawing a straight line between them.

Special-Purpose Maps

Maps that show part of the earth

For some uses, we would rather have maps that do not show the whole surface of the earth. A map of a very small part of the earth can be drawn more accurately than a map of a large area. It can also include more details.

Drawing I, on this page, shows a photograph and a map of the same small part of the earth. The drawings on the map that show the shape and location of things on the earth are called symbols. The small drawing that shows directions is called a compass* rose.

Maps for special purposes

Maps can show the location of many different kinds of things. For instance, a map can show what minerals are found in certain places, or what crops are grown. A small chart that lists the symbols and their meanings is usually included on a map. This is called the key.

Symbols on some geography maps stand for the amounts of things in different places. For instance, map J, at left, gives information about the number of people in the southwestern part of the United States. The key tells the meaning of the symbols. In this case the symbols are dots and circles.

On different maps, the same symbol may stand for different things and amounts.

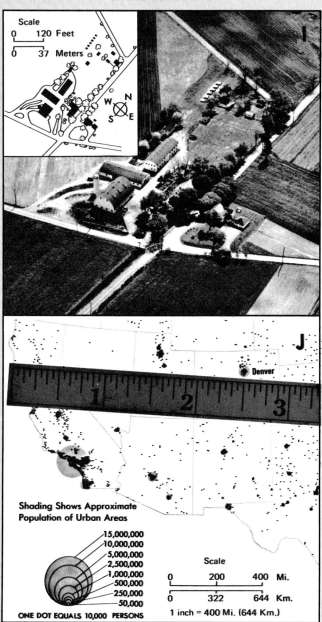

Each dot on map J stands for 10,000 persons. On other maps, a dot might represent 5,000 sheep or 1,000 bushels of wheat.

There are other ways of giving information about quantity. Different designs or patterns may be used on a rainfall map to show the areas that receive different amounts of rain each year.

Relief Maps

The roughness of the earth's surface

From a plane, you can see that the earth's surface is rough. You can see mountains and valleys, hills and plains. For some uses, globes and maps that show these things are needed. They are called relief globes and maps.

Since globes are three-dimensional* copies of the earth, you may wonder why most globes do not show the roughness of the earth's surface. The reason for this is that the highest mountain on the earth is not very large when it is compared with the earth's diameter. Even a very large globe would be smooth nearly everywhere.

In order to make a relief globe or map, you must use a different scale for the height of the land. You might start with a large flat map. One inch on your flat map may stand for a distance of 100 miles (161 kilometers) on the earth. Now you are going to make a small copy of a mountain on your map. On the earth, this mountain is two miles (3.2 kilometers) high. If you let one inch stand for this height on the earth, your mountain should rise one inch above the flat surface of your map. Other mountains and hills should be copied on this same scale.

By photographing relief globes and maps, flat maps can be made that show the earth much as it looks from an airplane. Map K, at right above, is a photograph of a relief map. Map L is a photograph of a relief globe.

Topographic maps

Another kind of map that shows the roughness of the earth's surface is called a topographic, or contour, map. On this kind of map, lines are drawn to show different heights of the earth's surface. These are

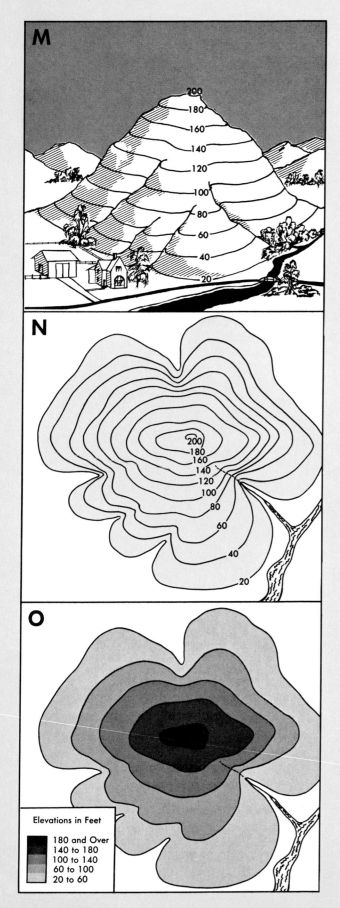

called contour lines. The maps on this page help to explain how topographic maps are made.

Map M is a drawing of a hill. Around the bottom of the hill is our first contour line. This line connects all the points at the base of the hill that are exactly twenty feet above sea level. Higher up the hill, another contour line is drawn. It connects all the points that are exactly forty feet above sea level. A line is also drawn at a height of sixty feet. Other lines are drawn every twenty feet until the top of the hill is reached. Since the hill is shaped somewhat like a cone, each contour line is shorter than the one just below it.

Map N shows how the contour lines in the drawing of the hill M can be used to make a topographic map. This map gives us a great deal of information about the hill. Since each line is labeled with the height it stands for, you can tell how high the different parts of the hill are. It is important to remember that land does not really rise in layers, as you might think when you look at a topographic map. Wherever the contour lines are far apart, you can be sure that the land slopes gently. Where they are close together, the slope is steep. With practice, you can picture the land in your mind as you look at such a map. Topographic maps are especially useful to people who design such things as roads and buildings.

On a topographic map, the spaces between the contour lines may be filled in with different shades of a color. If a different shade of brown were used for each different height of land shown in map N, there would be ten shades. It would be very hard for you to tell these different shades of brown apart. Therefore, on map O, at left, black and four shades of brown were used to show differences in height of forty feet. The key shows the height of the land represented by the different shades. On some topographic maps, different colors are used to stand for different heights.

Elevations in Feet

- 180 and Over
- 140 to 180
- 100 to 140
- 60 to 100
- 20 to 60

Presidents of the United States

No.	President	Home State	Years in Office	Political Party
1.	George Washington (1732-1799)	Virginia	1789-1797	(No party)
2.	John Adams (1735-1826)	Massachusetts	1797-1801	Federalist
3.	Thomas Jefferson (1743-1826)	Virginia	1801-1809	Democratic-Republican
4.	James Madison (1751-1836)	Virginia	1809-1817	Democratic-Republican
5.	James Monroe (1758-1831)	Virginia	1817-1825	Democratic-Republican
6.	John Quincy Adams (1767-1848)	Massachusetts	1825-1829	National Republican
7.	Andrew Jackson (1767-1845)	Tennessee	1829-1837	Democratic
8.	Martin Van Buren (1782-1862)	New York	1837-1841	Democratic
9.	William H. Harrison (1773-1841)	Ohio	March-April, 1841	Whig
10.	John Tyler (1790-1862)	Virginia	1841-1845	Whig
11.	James K. Polk (1795-1849)	Tennessee	1845-1849	Democratic
12.	Zachary Taylor (1784-1850)	Louisiana	1849-1850	Whig
13.	Millard Fillmore (1800-1874)	New York	1850-1853	Whig
14.	Franklin Pierce (1804-1869)	New Hampshire	1853-1857	Democratic
15.	James Buchanan (1791-1868)	Pennsylvania	1857-1861	Democratic
16.	Abraham Lincoln (1809-1865)	Illinois	1861-1865	Republican
17.	Andrew Johnson (1808-1875)	Tennessee	1865-1869	Republican
18.	Ulysses S. Grant (1822-1885)	Illinois	1869-1877	Republican
19.	Rutherford B. Hayes (1822-1893)	Ohio	1877-1881	Republican
20.	James A. Garfield (1831-1881)	Ohio	March-Sept., 1881	Republican
21.	Chester A. Arthur (1830-1886)	New York	1881-1885	Republican
22.	Grover Cleveland (1837-1908)	New York	1885-1889	Democratic
23.	Benjamin Harrison (1833-1901)	Indiana	1889-1893	Republican
24.	Grover Cleveland (1837-1908)	New York	1893-1897	Democratic
25.	William McKinley (1843-1901)	Ohio	1897-1901	Republican
26.	Theodore Roosevelt (1858-1919)	New York	1901-1909	Republican
27.	William Howard Taft (1857-1930)	Ohio	1909-1913	Republican
28.	Woodrow Wilson (1856-1924)	New Jersey	1913-1921	Democratic
29.	Warren G. Harding (1865-1923)	Ohio	1921-1923	Republican
30.	Calvin Coolidge (1872-1933)	Massachusetts	1923-1929	Republican
31.	Herbert Hoover (1874-1964)	California	1929-1933	Republican
32.	Franklin D. Roosevelt (1882-1945)	New York	1933-1945	Democratic
33.	Harry S. Truman (1884-1972)	Missouri	1945-1953	Democratic
34.	Dwight D. Eisenhower (1890-1969)	Pennsylvania	1953-1961	Republican
35.	John F. Kennedy (1917-1963)	Massachusetts	1961-1963	Democratic
36.	Lyndon B. Johnson (1908-1973)	Texas	1963-1969	Democratic
37.	Richard M. Nixon (1913-)	California	1969-1974	Republican
38.	Gerald R. Ford (1913-)	Michigan	1974-1977	Republican
39.	Jimmy E. Carter (1924-)	Georgia	1977-	Democratic

Our Needs

All people on earth must meet certain needs in order to be healthy and happy. Scientists who study human beings tell us that these basic needs are the same for everyone. It does not matter if you are rich or poor . . . tall or short . . . fat or thin . . . dark-skinned or light-skinned. You have the same basic needs as everyone else.

There are three kinds of basic needs. These are: physical needs, social needs, and the need for faith.

Physical Needs

Some basic needs are so important that people will die or become very sick if they are not able to meet them. These are called physical needs. Some of them are:

1. air
2. water
3. food
4. protection from heat and cold
5. sleep and rest
6. exercise

While all people share these needs, they do not all meet them in the same way. For example, some people protect themselves from the cold by living in houses made of wood or brick. Others live in houses of snow or in tents made from animal skins.

Social Needs

Even if you can meet all of your physical needs, you still may not be able to lead a happy and useful life. You must also meet certain other needs. Some of these are called social needs.

One of the most important social needs is to feel that you belong to a group. This group may be your family, your school, your church, or a group of friends. You need to feel that these people like you and respect you as a person.

Like most other people, you were born with certain abilities. For example, you may be able to make things with your hands or play a musical instrument. In order to be happy, you must develop and use your abilities as fully as possible.

Another social need is to have something important you want to accomplish. You must have goals. For example, you may decide to earn the money to buy a new bicycle. When you have earned this money, you have a feeling of satisfaction. Now you are ready to work toward other goals.

The Need for Faith

To have a happy life, every person needs something to believe in. For example, you need to have faith in yourself. You must believe that you can work toward solving whatever problems life brings to you. You also need to have faith in other people. You must be able to feel that you can count on them to do their part and to help you when you need help.

Most people also have some kind of religious faith. This can help people understand themselves and the world they live in. It can also help them live together happily. For example, most religions teach people to be honest and to love their neighbors.

Meeting Needs in Communities

No person can meet his or her needs all alone. Only by living and working with other people can a person have a happy, satisfying life. For this reason, people everywhere on earth have always lived in communities.

Over the years, people have followed certain ideas or ways of living that help them to live together in communities. We call these the "great ideas." In other parts of this book, you can discover how the great ideas have helped people in the United States to meet their basic needs.

Friends playing a game. How can friends help each other to meet their basic needs?

Word List
(Glossary)

Complete Pronunciation Key

Your study of this book will be more interesting if you take time to use this Glossary. You should turn to this Glossary each time a word that you read in the text is marked with an asterisk (*), unless you clearly understand the word. The pronunciation of each word is shown just after the word in this way: **Congress** (kong′ gris). The letters and signs used are pronounced as in the words below. The mark ′ is placed after a syllable with a primary or strong accent, as in the example above. The mark ′ after a syllable shows a secondary or lighter accent as in **conservation** (kon′ sər vā′ shən).

a	hat, cap	j	jam, enjoy	u	cup, butter	
ā	age, face	k	kind, seek	u̇	full, put	
ã	care, air	l	land, coal	ü	rule, move	
ä	father, far	m	me, am	ū	use, music	
		n	no, in			
b	bad, rob	ng	long, bring			
ch	child, much	o	hot, rock	v	very, save	
d	did, red	ō	open, go	w	will, woman	
		ô	order, all	y	young, yet	
e	let, best	oi	oil, voice	z	zero, breeze	
ē	equal, see	ou	house, out	zh	measure, seizure	
ėr	term, learn	p	paper, cup			
		r	run, try	ə	represents:	
f	fat, if	s	say, yes	a	in about	
g	go, bag	sh	she, rush	e	in taken	
h	he, how	t	tell, it	i	in pencil	
		th	thin, both	o	in lemon	
i	it, pin	ᴛʜ	then, smooth	u	in circus	
ī	ice, five					

amendment (ə mend′ mənt). A change in, or an addition to, a constitution or a law. See **constitution**.

American Philosophical (fil′ə sof′ə kl) **Society.** A society, or club, started by Benjamin Franklin in 1743. He wanted to bring scientists and other educated people in the colonies together. Today, the members of this society include hundreds of well-known scientists from the United States and other countries. See **scientists**.

antislavery (an′tē slāv′ər ē). Against slavery. See **slavery**.

anvil (an′vəl). A block of iron or steel, used by a blacksmith to shape metal. (See picture on pages 98-99 of *Great Ideas*.)

Appalachian (ap′ə lā′chən) **Mountains.** A large group of mountains in the eastern part of our country. These mountains extend from central Alabama northeast into Canada.

apprentice (ə pren′ tis). A person who is learning a job by working under the direction of a skilled worker.

arrest. To take someone who appears to have broken a law to court or to jail. For example, a police officer might arrest someone for robbing a bank.

astronaut (as′ trə nôt). A pilot or a crew member of a spacecraft.

bifocal (bī fō′ kl) **glasses.** Eyeglasses with two sections for each eye. The top part is for looking at things far away. The bottom part is for looking at things close up. Before Franklin invented bifocal glasses, many persons had to use two different pairs of glasses.

birchbark. The bark of the birch tree. It is easily peeled off in large pieces.

bomb. A weapon that explodes.

Braddock, Edward, 1695-1755. A British general. Braddock was in charge of British soldiers in America during the French and Indian War. He was killed in a battle of this war in 1755. See **French and Indian War.**

Buddhist (bùd′ ist). A follower of the religion of Buddhism. This religion was started by Siddhartha Gautama Buddha about 2,500 years ago. It is followed by millions of people in Japan and other Asian countries.

cable (kā′ bl). A thick rope made of wires that carry electricity.

calculator (kal′ kyə lā′ tər). A machine that is used to add, subtract, multiply, and divide.

candidate (kan′ də dāt). A person who is trying to get elected to a job or an office, such as president. Each candidate in an election hopes to get the most votes.

Cape Canaveral (kə nav′ ə rəl). An area on the east coast of Florida where the John F. Kennedy Space Center is located. From 1963 to 1973, Cape Canaveral was called Cape Kennedy.

Celsius (sel′sē əs). Refers to a scale for measuring temperature. On the Celsius scale, which is part of the metric system, 0° represents the freezing point of water and 100° represents the boiling point. To change degrees Celsius to degrees on the Fahrenheit scale, multiply by 1.8 and add 32. See **metric system** and **Fahrenheit.**

charcoal. A substance made by partly burning wood in an oven from which the air has been shut out. Charcoal is usually black or dark brown. It is used as a fuel.

chemicals (kem′ ə klz). Substances that are made when two or more substances act upon one another. Examples are salt, soda, ammonia, and aspirin.

Chippewa (chip′ ə wä). An Indian tribe that once lived along the shores of Lake Superior. Today many Chippewa live in Michigan, Minnesota, and Wisconsin. Others live in Ontario, Canada.

Christianity (kris′ chē an′ ə tē). A religion that is followed by more people than any other religion in the world. It is based on the teachings of Jesus Christ, who lived nearly two thousand years ago. There are three main branches of Christianity. These are the Roman Catholic Church, the Eastern Orthodox churches, and the Protestant churches.

circumference (sər kum′fər əns). The distance around something, such as a circle or a ball.

civil rights. The rights and freedoms that belong to a person as a member of a community, a state, or a country. There are many different civil rights. Among them are the right to speak freely and to attend the church of one's choice. Others are the right to own property, the right to a fair trial, and the right to get a job or a place to live. Sometimes the right to vote is also thought of as a civil right.

Civil War, 1861-1865. A war between the northern and southern parts of our country. The northern states were called the Union. The southern states were called the Confederacy. The Union won the Civil War.

colonial (kə lō′ nē əl). Refers to a certain period of time in the history of the United States. The colonial period began when the first European colonies were started in America. It lasted until the thirteen British colonies became the United States in 1776.

colony (kol′ ə nē). A settlement outside the country that controls it. In American history, it usually means any one of thirteen British colonies along the Atlantic coast. These colonies were started by people from Europe in the 1600's and 1700's. Later, the thirteen colonies became the United States.

communicate (kə mū′ nə kāt). To share ideas and feelings with other people. Speaking and writing are two of the most important ways of communicating.

communications (kə mū′ nə kā′ shənz). Different ways of communicating over a distance. For example, telephones and radio are part of the communications industry. See **communicate.**

community (kə mū′ nə tē). A group of people who live in the same place and have the same laws.

compass rose. A small drawing put on a map to show directions. Here are three examples of compass roses:

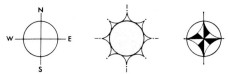

computer (kəm pūt′ ər). A machine that stores information and uses this information to solve difficult problems.

Congress (kong′ gris). A group of people who are elected to make the laws for the United States. Congress is made up of two parts, or houses. These are the Senate and the House of Representatives.

conservation (kon′ sər vā′ shən). Saving or protecting something so it will not be wasted. For example, forests and soil need to be conserved.

constitution (kon′ stə tü′ shən). A set of rules telling how a country or a state is supposed to be governed. When this word is written with a capital "C," it usually means the Constitution of the United States. Our Constitution was adopted in 1788. It has been in use ever since.

continent (kont′ n ənt). One of the six largest land areas on the earth. These are Eurasia, Africa, North America, South America, Australia, and Antarctica. Some people think of Eurasia as two continents—Europe and Asia.

Continental (kont′ n en′ tl) **Congress.** A meeting of leaders from the colonies in America that later joined together to form the

---

PRONUNCIATION KEY: hat, āge, cãre, fär; let, ēqual, tėrm; it, īce; hot, ōpen, ôrder; oil, out; cup, pùt, rüle, ūse; child; long; thin; ŦHen; zh, measure; ə represents a in about, e in taken, i in pencil, o in lemon, u in circus. For the complete key, see page 132.

United States. There were two Continental Congresses. The First Continental Congress met in 1774 to discuss the quarrel between the colonies and Great Britain. The Second Continental Congress met in 1775, soon after the Revolutionary War began. On July 4, 1776, it approved the Declaration of Independence. For several years after this, the Second Continental Congress served as the government of the United States.

courage (kėr′ ij). The ability to face something dangerous or unpleasant without fear. Bravery.

courageous (kə rā′ jəs). Having courage. See **courage**.

cradle. A kind of tool once used to cut grain. It had a blade fastened to a curved wooden handle. Next to the blade was a wooden framework to gather the grain. A person using a cradle swept the blade along just above the ground. The cut grain fell onto the framework.

debate (di bāt′). A public discussion or argument about some important question. In a debate, there are two or more persons who give different points of view.

Declaration (dek′ lə rā′ shən) **of Independence.** A public statement made by leaders of the American colonies on July 4, 1776. This statement said that the colonies were independent, or free, of Great Britain.

democracy (di mok′ rə sē). A country in which people govern themselves. The people choose their leaders and make decisions by majority vote. See **majority**.

democratic (dem ′ə krat′ik). Refers to a country in which the people choose their leaders and make decisions by voting. See **democracy**.

demonstrate (dem′ ən strāt). To show or explain. Sometimes, to meet with other people in public to show one's feelings about something.

deposit (di poz′ it). A mass of a useful substance, such as gravel or coal. A deposit may be on the earth's surface or underneath it.

depression (di presh′ ən). A time when many people are out of work and businesses are not able to make much money.

diameter (dī am′ ə tər). A straight line that joins opposite sides and passes through the center of something, such as a circle or a ball. Also, the length of such a straight line.

dictator (dik′ tā tər). A ruler who has complete power over the people of a country.

Eastern Orthodox (ôr′ thə doks). Refers to one of the three main branches of Christianity. (See **Christianity**.) Most of the churches that belong to this branch are in western Asia and eastern Europe. The term Eastern Orthodox also refers to members of Eastern Orthodox churches.

Eastern Woodlands. An area in the eastern part of North America. It extends from Tennessee and Virginia northward into Canada. Long ago, this area was covered with thick forests.

economic (ē′ kə nom′ik). Having to do with earning a living.

elect. To choose a person for a job by voting. Usually the person who receives the most votes gets the job.

election. The choosing of someone for a job or a government office by voting.

Emancipation (i man′ sə pā′ shən) **Proclamation** (prok′ lə mā′ shən). A public statement made by President Lincoln on January 1, 1863. This proclamation freed the slaves in the parts of the Confederacy that were still fighting against the Union. See **Civil War.**

energy. Power, or force, that can be used to do work. In earliest times, people used only their own muscles to do work. Since then, they have learned to use many other sources of energy. Among these are wind, flowing water, and fuels such as coal, oil, and natural gas.

epidemic (ep′ ə dem′ ik). An outbreak of a disease. In an epidemic, many people have the same disease at the same time.

experiment (eks per′ ə ment). A test planned to discover facts about nature or to help decide whether or not something is true. Also, a test to see if a new idea will work.

Fahrenheit (far′ ən hīt). Refers to a scale for measuring temperature in which the freezing point of water is represented by 32° and the boiling point by 212°. See **Celsius.**

fertilizer (fėr′tl īz′ər). A substance that farmers add to their soil. The fertilizer helps the soil produce more and better crops.

fiber. A thread or threadlike part.

flatboat. A boat with a flat bottom and square ends, used on rivers and canals.

flax. A plant with small leaves and blue flowers. The stem of this plant can be separated into fibers. (See **fiber.**) Cloth made from the fibers of the flax plant is called linen.

Franklin stove. An iron stove for heating a room. It looks something like an open fireplace, but it is not built into a wall. For this reason, it spreads heat in all directions.

French and Indian War, 1754-1763. A war in North America. In this war, Great Britain and its American colonies defeated the French. Indians fought on both sides. As a result of the war, Great Britain took over most of the land that the French had owned in North America.

frontier (frun tir′). An area that lies between settled lands and the wilderness.

Great Britain (brit′ n). A large island that lies off the western coast of Europe. It is made up of three parts—England, Scotland, and Wales. Long ago, these were three countries with different rulers. Wales was joined to England during the 1500's. Then, in 1707, England and Wales were united with Scotland to form the kingdom of Great Britain. The ruler of Great Britain also ruled the British colonies in America. Later, the northern part of Ireland became part of the kingdom of Great Britain. Today, the official name for this country is "The United Kingdom of Great Britain and Northern Ireland."

great circle. Any imaginary line around the earth that divides it exactly in half. The equator, for example, is a great circle. The shortest route between any two points on the earth always lies on the great circle that passes through them.

Great Lakes. Five huge lakes in the central part of North America. These are Lakes Superior, Michigan, Huron, Erie, and Ontario.

Great Plains. A part of our country that is made up of broad, level plains. It lies east of the Rocky Mountains and extends from Canada to Mexico.

Gutenberg (güt'n bėrg), **Johann,** 1400?-?1468. A German inventor and printer.

Hindu (hin' dü). A follower of the religion of Hinduism. Hinduism is the main religion in India and several other parts of Asia. Hindus are divided into many groups, which have different customs and worship different gods.

Hopi (hō' pē). An Indian tribe that now lives in northeastern Arizona.

House of Representatives (rep' ri zen' tə tivs). One of the two lawmaking groups that make up the Congress of the United States. The other lawmaking group is called the Senate. There are 435 members in the House of Representatives. The number of representatives from each state depends on the number of people living in the state.

human being. A person. The term "human beings" refers to people when they are thought of as different from animals.

hypodermic (hī pə dėr' mik) **needle.** A hollow needle used to put medicine or vaccine under a person's skin. See **vaccine.**

immunity (i mū' nə tē). The ability to keep from getting a certain disease. For example, a person who has had chicken pox usually will not get that disease again. We say that this person has an immunity to chicken pox.

inaugural (in ô' gyə rəl). Refers to the beginning of a person's new term of office. May also refer to the speech given by such a person.

independent (in' di pen' dənt). Free from control by another country.

inferior (in fir' ē ər). Not as good as someone or something else.

inherit (in her' it). To receive something of value from a person who dies. For example, children often inherit money from their parents.

inoculate (in ok' yə lāt). To give a person a mild form of a disease by a shot of dead or weakened germs. Inoculation keeps the person from getting a more serious form of the disease.

invent. To think up something useful and make it for the first time.

ironworks. A building or group of buildings in which iron or iron objects are made.

Jew. A member of a group of people held together for more than three thousand years by their history and their religious faith. The history of the Jews began in southwestern Asia, probably about 1900 B.C. The Jewish faith, called Judaism, is one of the world's major religions. The main beliefs of Judaism are that there is only one God, that God is good, and that God wants people to follow his laws. Two other major religions, Christianity and Islam, grew out of Judaism.

jury (jùr' ē). A group of persons who serve in a court of law. The jury studies the facts and decides whether or not the person charged with a crime is guilty.

kilometer (kə lom' ə tər). A unit in the metric system for measuring length. It is equal to about .62 mile. See **metric system.**

Korean (kô rē' ən) **War,** 1950-1953. A war between North Korea and South Korea, two countries in eastern Asia. The United

Nations sent soldiers to help South Korea. Many of these soldiers were Americans. See **United Nations.**

labor union. A group of workers who join together to reach certain goals. For example, a labor union may try to get a company to pay more money to its workers.

Latin school. In colonial times a school that prepared boys for college. It was called a Latin school because boys who planned to go to college had to learn Latin. Latin was the language of the ancient Romans in Europe.

legislature (lej′ is lā′ chər). A group of persons who have the power to make laws for a state or a country.

lightning rod. A metal rod set up on a building or a ship. Its purpose is to lead lightning from the sky into the ground or the water. This keeps the lightning from starting a fire or doing other damage.

livestock. Farm animals such as cattle, hogs, sheep, horses, and chickens.

loyal. Faithful. You may be loyal to a person or a group of persons, such as your government. You may also be loyal to an idea.

loyalty. Faithfulness. See **loyal.**

majority (mə jôr′ ə tē). Usually, any number over half. The term "majority vote" refers to a way in which groups of people make decisions. In this system, important questions are decided and people are elected to office by the largest number of votes.

Marconi (mär kō′ nē), **Guglielmo,** 1874-1937. An Italian inventor.

Medal of Freedom. See **Presidential Medal of Freedom.**

metal type. Pieces of metal with raised letters or numbers. Used for printing books, newspapers, and magazines.

metric system. A system of measurement used in many countries throughout the world, especially in science. In this system, the meter is the basic unit of length.

microscope (mī′ krə skōp). A tool used by scientists for making very tiny things look larger.

Middle Colonies. Four of the thirteen British colonies along the Atlantic coast of North America. These were New York, Pennsylvania, New Jersey, and Delaware. See **colony.**

mineral (min′ ər əl). Any of certain substances found in the earth. Diamonds and coal are examples of minerals.

minister (min′ is tər). A person who leads church services and gives talks, called sermons, to the members of the church. Also, a person sent by his or her government to the government of another country to carry out official business.

Moslem (moz′ ləm). A follower of Islam, a religion founded by Mohammed more than 1,300 years ago. Moslems believe that there is only one God, and that Mohammed is God's prophet. Large numbers of Moslems live in northern Africa and southwestern Asia.

natural gas. A kind of gas found beneath the surface of the earth. It is used mainly as a fuel.

PRONUNCIATION KEY: hat, āge, cãre, fär; let, ēqual, tėrm; it, īce; hot, ōpen, ôrder; oil, out; cup, pùt, rüle, ūse; child; long; thin; ᴛHen; zh, measure; ə represents a in about, e in taken, i in pencil, o in lemon, u in circus. For the complete key, see page 132.

natural resources. Useful things found in nature, such as soil, water, trees, and minerals. See **mineral.**

New England. An area in the northeastern part of our country. Four of the thirteen British colonies along the Atlantic coast were in New England. (See **colony.**) These were Massachusetts, New Hampshire, Connecticut, and Rhode Island. Today, New England includes these four states plus Maine and Vermont.

Nobel (nō bel*'*) **Peace Prize.** A prize given almost every year to a person who has worked for peaceful solutions to important problems.

noble (nō*'* bl). A high-ranking person such as a prince, a duke, or a duchess. Usually people are nobles because their parents were nobles also. They enjoy a number of special privileges that other people in their country do not have. The United States does not have any nobles.

nonfiction (non fik*'* shən). Writing that deals with real people and events.

ore. Rock or other material that contains enough metal to make it worth mining.

patchwork quilt. A warm covering for a bed. The top is made from patches of cloth of different colors and shapes. These have been sewed together.

petition (pə tish*'* ən). A written request sent to a government official, a lawmaking group, or a court. To petition means to send such a request.

petroleum (pə trō*'* lē əm). Also called oil. A thick oily liquid that comes from the earth. Petroleum may be dark brown or greenish black in color. Gasoline and many other useful things are made from petroleum.

Pilgrims. A group of English colonists who came to America in 1620. The Pilgrims had left England because they had not been allowed to worship God as they pleased. They started a colony called Plymouth in what is now Massachusetts.

planet. The earth or any other heavenly body that moves around the sun. The nine main planets are Mercury, Venus, Earth, Mars, Jupiter, Saturn, Uranus, Neptune, and Pluto.

plantation. A large farm where a crop such as cotton, tobacco, or sugarcane is raised. The workers usually live on the plantation.

polio. A short form of the word poliomyelitis. This is a serious disease that causes fever and weakness of the muscles. Some people die from polio and some become lame.

political (pə lit*'* ə kl). Having to do with citizens or government.

pollution (pə lü*'* shən). Making something dirty. For example, air or water may become polluted.

prejudice (prej*'* ə dis). An opinion that is formed without knowing all the facts. The dislike for a person just because he or she belongs to a different group is a common kind of prejudice.

president (prez*'* ə dənt). The leader of an organization such as a club, a business, or a government. The president of the United States is the head of our government and sees that our country's laws are carried out.

Presidential (prez*'* ə den*'* shəl) **Medal of Freedom.** An important award given to citizens who are not members of our armed forces.

printing press. A machine that can print many copies of a book, newspaper, or magazine in a short time.

profit. The money earned by a business. It is the amount of money taken in, minus the money spent in running the business.

property. Things that people own, such as land, buildings, animals, and money.

Protestant (prot′ is tənt). Refers to one of the three main branches of Christianity. (See **Christianity**.) Also, a member of any one of the many different Protestant groups, such as the Methodists, Baptists, or Presbyterians.

pulp. A soft, damp material usually made from wood or rags. It is used in making paper.

Quaker (kwāk′ ər). A member of a religious group called the Society of Friends. This group was started in England by George Fox about 1650.

racial (rā′ shəl). Having to do with a person's race, such as black, white, or Asian.

refinery (ri fīn′ ər ē). A place where useful products are made from something found in nature. For example, petroleum is made into gasoline, kerosene, and other useful products in a refinery.

research (ri serch′). A careful search for facts or truth about a subject.

reservation (rez′ ər vā′ shən). An area of land owned by the government and set aside for some special use. Especially, an area set aside for use by Indians.

responsibility (ri spon′ sə bil′ ə tē). Duty. Something that a person ought to do because it is the right thing to do, such as obeying the law.

Revolutionary (rev′ ə lü′ shən er′ ē) **War,** 1775-1783. A war between Great Britain and thirteen British colonies in America. The colonies won the war and became states in a new country. This was the United States.

Roman Catholic. Refers to a church that is one of the three main branches of Christianity. Also refers to members of this church. See **Christianity**.

satellite (sat′ l īt). A heavenly body that circles around a larger body in space. For example, the moon is a satellite of the earth. Objects called satellites have also been made by people. Most of these circle the earth and send back useful information. Some of them give us facts about the weather. Other satellites send television programs to many parts of the earth.

scalping. Taking the skin and hair off part of a person's head.

scientist. An expert in some branch of science. A scientist makes an orderly study of natural laws and facts about nature.

Second Continental Congress. See **Continental Congress.**

Senate. One of the two lawmaking groups that make up the Congress of the United States. The other lawmaking group is called the House of Representatives. There are 100 members in the Senate, two from each state in our country.

PRONUNCIATION KEY: hat, āge, cāre, fär; let, ēqual, tėrm; it, īce; hot, ōpen, ôrder; oil, out; cup, put, rüle, ūse; child; long; thin; ŦHen; zh, measure; ə represents a in about, e in taken, i in pencil, o in lemon, u in circus. For the complete key, see page 132.

sermon. A talk given as part of a church service. A sermon usually tells people about religion or how they should behave.

Sioux (sü). An Indian tribe in the central part of North America.

slavery. The custom of owning slaves.

slum. A crowded, run-down part of a city or town. Most of the people who live in slums are very poor.

smallpox. A serious disease from which many people once died.

solar system. The sun together with the nine main planets and other heavenly bodies that move around it. See **planet.**

Southern Colonies. Five of the thirteen British colonies along the Atlantic coast of North America. These were Maryland, Virginia, North Carolina, South Carolina, and Georgia. See **colony.**

Southwest. A large area in the southwestern part of our country. It includes the states of Arizona and New Mexico.

Stamp Act. A law passed by the British government in 1765 to raise money. This law said that all American newspapers and other documents had to be stamped. In some cases, the documents were printed on stamped paper, but stamps were also sold separately. Both the stamped paper and the stamps had to be bought from colonial agents of the British government.

steam engine. An engine that is run by steam. To produce the steam, water is heated by burning a fuel such as coal or oil. Steam engines are often used to run trains and ships. They are also used in power plants to produce electricity.

Supreme (sə prēm′) **Court.** The most important court of law in the United States. It meets in the nation's capital, Washington, D.C. The Supreme Court has nine judges, who are called justices. Their job is to make sure that our country is being governed according to the rules in the Constitution. See **constitution.**

surrender (sə ren′ dər). To give up something to another person or to a group of people. For example, the general in charge of one army might surrender to the general of an enemy army.

survey (sər vā′). To find out the exact location and size of a piece of land.

symbol (sim′ bl). Something that stands for, or represents, something else. For example, the American flag represents the United States.

textile (teks′ tl). Cloth, or the thread used to make cloth.

three-dimensional (də men′ shə nəl). Refers to anything that has height, length, and width.

tomahawk. A small ax used by North American Indians as a weapon or a tool.

tragedy (traj′ ə dē). A very sad or terrible happening.

treaty (trē′ tē). An agreement, usually in writing, between two or more nations.

Union. The United States of America. During the Civil War, the northern states were called the Union. See **Civil War.**

United Nations. An organization of countries from all over the world. It was started in 1945 to work for world peace. About 150 countries now belong to the United Nations.

United States House of Representatives. See **House of Representatives.**

United States Senate. See **Senate.**

university (ū′ nə vėr′ sə tē). A kind of school that students may attend after finishing high school. A university is made up of several parts called schools or colleges. For example, a university may include schools of law, medicine, and business.

vaccine (vak′ sēn). The material used to inoculate a person. See **inoculate.**

vessel. A dish or pan. Bowls, cups, pitchers, and kettles are different kinds of vessels.

victim. A person who is harmed by something or someone.

violence (vī′ ə ləns). The use of force to harm someone or to cause damage to something.

virus (vī′ rəs). Any of certain kinds of germs that cause diseases such as colds and chicken pox.

women's rights. Civil rights for women. See **civil rights.**

World War II, 1939-1945. A war that was fought in many parts of the world. On one side were the Allies. These included the United States, Great Britain, the Soviet Union, France, and many other countries. On the other side were the Axis Powers, which included Germany, Italy, and Japan. The Allies defeated the Axis Powers.

Acknowledgments
(Great Ideas)

Grateful acknowledgment is made to the following for permission to use the illustrations found in this book:

A. Devaney, Inc.: Pages 76-77 by Josef Scaylea
Alpha Photo Associates, Inc.: Pages 1 and 103
American Museum of Natural History: Pages 96-97
American Telephone and Telegraph: Page 57
Authenticated News International: Page 79
Barbara Versluis: Pages 60-61
Bethlehem Steel: Pages 74-75, painting by S.B. Shiley
Black Star: Page 39 by Charles Moore; pages 46-47 by Arnold Zann; pages 70-71 by Dan J. McCoy; pages 100-101 by Joseph S. Rychetnik; page 108 by Christopher Springmann
Boatman's National Bank: Pages 6-7, painting by George Caleb Bingham
Camerique: Pages 20, 22-23, and 102
Carlberg Photographic: Pages 36-37
Colonial Williamsburg: Pages 34, 55, and 98-99
De Wys: Page 105
Editorial Photocolor Archives: Page 12 by Eugene Luttenberg; page 69 by Laima Turnley
Frederic Lewis: Page 93
Freelance Photographers Guild: Page 85
Grand Rapids Public Schools: Page 45
Grant Heilman: Pages 17 and 82-83; page 38 by Runk/Schoenberger; page 80 by Alan Pitcairn
H. Armstrong Roberts: Pages 15, 21, 50-51, 70, 104, and 112
Harold Lambert Studios: Page 50
Historical Pictures Service: Page 92
Hull House Association: Pages 42-43 and 43
John Hancock Mutual Life Insurance Co.: Pages 14-15 and 67

Ken Heyman: Pages 13, 26-27, 48-49, 58-59, 94-95, and 109
Library of Congress: Page 35
M. E. Warren: Pages 10-11, painting by Francis Blackwell Mager
Magnum Photos, Inc.: Page 8 by Mark Godfrey; page 16 by Paul Fusco; page 27 by Alex Webb; page 49 by Erich Hartmann; pages 68-69 by Lawrence Fried; page 131 by Burk Uzzle
NASA: Page 28
N.C.R. Corporation: Pages 2-3
National Life Insurance Co.: Page 99
North American Aviation, Inc.: Page 30
North American Rockwell: Page 31
St. Louis Art Museum: Pages 64-65
The Fideler Co.: Pages 32-33, 62-63, 72-73, 74, 86-87, 89, 90-91, 106-107; pages 52-53, 56-57, and 88 by Marian Schuhman
The White House: Pages 4-5
United Airlines: Pages 110-111
United States Capitol Historical Society: Pages 24-25 by George F. Mobley, National Geographic photographer
United States Department of Agriculture: Pages 18-19, 19, and 84
United States Department of Interior, Bureau of Reclamation: Pages 80-81 by F. B. Slote
Valley Forge Historical Society: Pages 40-41 by William T. Trego
Van Cleve Photography: Page 9

Index

(Great Ideas)

Explanation of abbreviations used in this Index: *p* — picture   *m* — map

---

PRONUNCIATION KEY: hat, āge, cãre, fär; let, ēqual, tėrm; it, īce; hot, ōpen, ôrder; oil, out; cup, pu̇t, rüle, u̇se; child; long**; thin; ᴛʜen; zh, measure; ə represents a in about, e in taken, i in pencil, o in lemon, u in circus. For the complete key, see page 132.**